PhotoPlus X2 Resource Guide

This book has been created and output in entirety using Serif PagePlus

How to contact us

Contacting Serif Technical Support:

Our support mission is to provide fast, friendly technical advice and support from a team of on-call experts. Technical support is provided from our Web support page, and useful information can be obtained via our web-based forums (see below). There are no pricing policies after the 30 day money back guarantee period.

UK/International/US   **http://www.serif.com/support**
Technical Support

Additional Serif contact information:

Web:
Serif Web Site   **http://www.serif.com**
Forums   **http://www.serif.com/forums.asp**

Our main office (UK, Europe):
The Software Centre
PO Box 2000, Nottingham, NG11 7GW, UK

Main	(0115) 914 2000
Registration (UK only)	(0800) 376 1989
Sales (UK only)	(0800) 376 7070
Technical Support (UK only)	(0845) 345 6770
Customer Service (UK/International)	**http://www.serif.com/support**
General Fax	(0115) 914 2020

American office (USA, Canada):
The Software Center
13 Columbia Drive, Suite 5, Amherst NH 03031, USA

Main	(603) 889-8650
Registration	(800) 794-6876
Sales	(800) 55-SERIF or 557-3743
Customer Service	**http://www.serif.com/support**
General Fax	(603) 889-1127

International
Please contact our main office.

PhotoPlus X2 Resource Guide

Contents

Introduction

Welcome to the *PhotoPlus X2 Resource Guide*—whether you are new to PhotoPlus or a seasoned professional, the *Resource Guide* offers content to help you get the best out of PhotoPlus. From a range of novice and professional tutorials to get you started or to help accomplish a complex project, to full-colour previews of PhotoPlus's Macros, Brushes, and the Image Collection available on the *Studio Extras* DVD, the *Resource Guide* is something you'll return to time and time again.

About the Guide

The *Resource Guide* is your key to getting even more out of PhotoPlus and is organized into the following chapters.

- **Tutorials**—Step-by-step training covering the basics of using PhotoPlus and how to tackle some interesting projects.
- **Design Projects**—More advanced training in the form of fully-fledged projects.
- **Makeover Studio**—Includes professional retouching effects such as teeth whitening, skin smoothing, dark circle reduction, and more.
- **Macros**—PhotoPlus X2 has the power to do all the hard work for you.
- **Brushes**—Brush Tips and Picture Brushes: what they are and how to use them!
- **Image Collection**—A collection of 500 images available to you on the *Studio Extras* DVD!

How the Resource Guide was made!

This full-colour *Resource Guide* was created and output using PagePlus X2, employing many features including BookPlus to unify separate publications with a common page numbering system; Mail and Photo Merge with Repeating Areas to automatically create pages with picture content based on a folder of images; and Find and Replace functionality to apply text styles consistently (and quickly) throughout. *Resource Guide* content based on PhotoPlus X2 object attributes, such as fonts and object styles, uses real PhotoPlus text and objects along with the attributes shown.

Finally, each chapter has been incorporated into a PagePlus Book comprised of multiple publication "chapters" and has been published as a press-ready PDF, accurately maintaining all text, fonts, images, and native colouring, all in a suitable CMYK colour format for professional printing. Be sure to read the "Tutorials" chapter for more information about PagePlus's powerful new features!

Tutorials

1

Introduction

Welcome to the PhotoPlus X2 tutorials!

Each tutorial provides illustrated, step-by-step instructions to show you how to get from the initial image to the end result.

You can apply the techniques demonstrated in the tutorials to your own photographs and images. If you prefer, however, you can use the sample images provided in your **Tutorials/Workspace** folder.

In a default installation, this folder is installed to the following location:

C:\Program Files\Serif\PhotoPlus\X2\Tutorials\Workspace

The tutorials are divided into four categories:

Getting Started

Aimed at new users, the Getting Started sequence steps you through the basic photo editing workflow—from getting your images in to PhotoPlus, right through to printing them out. Along the way, you'll use various tools and techniques to resize your images and correct some of the more common photo editing problems.

Basics

The Basics sequence introduces new users to foundation concepts and basic PhotoPlus features. Learn about colour spaces, images formats, selection tools, and more.

Photography

In the Photography section, you'll find a selection of tutorials aimed at helping you get the most out of your digital images. Whether you want to restore an old or damaged photo, add colour to a black and white image, or replace a photo background, you're sure to find something here that interests you.

Creative Effects

If you want to try something a little different, dip into the Creative Effects section and learn how PhotoPlus effects can be used to turn your images into art.

> To access PDF versions of the tutorials, click **Help**, then **View Tutorials**. To quickly switch back and forth between PhotoPlus and the tutorial document use the **Alt+Tab** keyboard shortcut.

Getting Started

New to PhotoPlus and photo editing? These exercises will step you through the basic photo editing workflow.

- **Getting Images into PhotoPlus**
- **Changing Image and Canvas Size**
- **Making Basic Image Corrections**
- **Sharpening Images**
- **Printing Photographs**

Getting Images Into PhotoPlus

In this tutorial, we'll show you how to browse and open your existing image files, and how to acquire images directly from your scanner or TWAIN-compliant digital camera.

Once you've opened your image files, we'll show you how to use some new PhotoPlus features that allow you to work on multiple images simultaneously.

You'll learn how to:

- Open existing images from the Startup Wizard.

- Open existing images from the File menu.

- Use the PhotoPlus Image Browser.

- Acquire images directly from your TWAIN-compatible scanner or digital camera.

- Use the new PhotoPlus Documents tab and image comparison options.

Getting Images Into PhotoPlus

PhotoPlus supports images saved in a wide variety of industry-standard file formats—TIFF, PNG, JPEG, GIF, PCX, as well as RAW (unprocessed) image data files captured by digital cameras. The following pages discuss the main concepts and techniques you need to know.

Opening and browsing existing images

PhotoPlus supports all the standard image formats for print and Web graphics, in addition to its native .SPP format. There are a number of different methods to access and open your existing image files.

- You can use the PhotoPlus **Startup Wizard** to open image files recently viewed in PhotoPlus, or to browse your computer for other image files.

- You can use the **File** menu to select and open a recently opened file, or to open a standard **Open** dialog.

- You can use the **Image Browser** to browse thumbnails of the images saved, which automatically creates thumbnails for images in the folders you open.

To open images from the Startup Wizard

1 From the PhotoPlus Startup Wizard, click **open saved work**.

In the **Open Saved Work** dialog, the left pane displays files you've recently worked on. (The first time you open PhotoPlus this pane will be empty.)

2 Select a recent image from the list and click **Finish**.

- or -

Click the **Browse** button to browse for other images in the **Open** dialog.

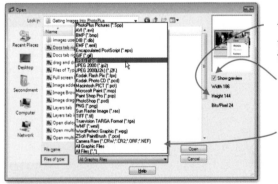

The **Open** dialog displays the dimensions and bit depth for the selected image.

- To display image thumbnails, select the **Show preview** option.

- To filter the list of file types shown in the dialog, select from the **Files of type** list.

Select the file you want to open and then click **Open**.

Getting Images Into PhotoPlus

Opening multiple files

- To open multiple adjacent files, select the first file in the list, press and hold down the **Shift** key, and then select the last file.

- To open multiple non-adjacent files, press and hold down the **Ctrl** key and then click to select the files you want to open.

To open images from the File menu

1 From the **File** menu, click **Open**. (You can also click the **Open** button on the Standard toolbar.)

2 In the **Open** dialog, select the file(s) you want to open.

- To open multiple files, press the **Ctrl** or **Shift** key when selecting their names.

- To display a thumbnail of each image as its filename is selected, select the **Show preview** option. See illustration on previous page.

3 Click **Open** to open the desired image in a separate image window.

As a shortcut from either Windows Explorer or the Image Browser (discussed later), you can simply drag and drop an image file icon or preview thumbnail into PhotoPlus.

- To create a **new layer** from a dragged image, drop the image file icon into the current window.

- To open a **new image** window, drop onto a blank region within the main workspace.

Once you've opened an image:

- To create an instant working copy in a new window, click **Image**, then **Duplicate**.

- To revert to the saved version of the current image, click **File**, then **Revert**.

Capturing digital camera RAW data files

PhotoPlus will also open the increasingly popular 'RAW' file formats.

An image saved in RAW format is the digital equivalent to the exposed film negative—the uncompressed, unprocessed data captured before any in-camera processing is applied.

The settings you choose to apply to your image (image quality, zoom, saturation, contrast, sharpening, and so on) are saved in a separate header file associated with the RAW data. When these settings are applied to the RAW data, the result is a processed and compressed JPEG image, which is written to the camera's memory card.

If you require ultimate control over your image adjustments and settings, or if you intend to print a certain picture extra large, RAW file format is the answer. Generally, however, saving in JPEG is more than adequate for most photographers' needs.

Getting Images Into PhotoPlus

Once you've opened PhotoPlus, you can use the built-in image browser to preview thumbnails and access file information for images stored in folders. The image browser automatically generates the thumbnails as you browse, and can retain (cache) the thumbnail gallery files for faster previewing next time around.

To use the image browser

1 From the **File** menu, choose **Image Browser**. (To browse the contents of the *Studio Extras DVD*, choose **Browse Creative Resources**.)

2 In the left pane of the Browse window, use the folder view to browse directories and files just as you would in Windows Explorer.

On the right, a thumbnail gallery displays images saved in the currently selected folder.

3 To open an image in a new PhotoPlus window, right-click the image thumbnail and then click **Open**.

- or -

Drag and drop its thumbnail into PhotoPlus.

(You can use the same drag-and-drop technique using file icons directly from Windows Explorer.)

- If you drop an image onto a blank region in the main PhotoPlus workspace, the image opens in a new window.

- If you drop an image onto an open image window, the new image is added to the existing document as a new layer.

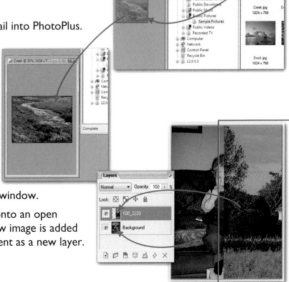

Getting Images Into PhotoPlus

Acquiring a TWAIN image

If your scanner or digital camera supports the industry-wide TWAIN standard, you can bring pictures from these devices directly into PhotoPlus.

If you have more than one TWAIN-compatible device installed, you may first need to select which source to use.

> To set up your TWAIN device for importing, see the documentation supplied with the device.

To select a TWAIN source for scanning

1 From the **File** menu, select **Import**, and then click **Select Source**.

2 In the **Select Source** dialog, click the device and then click **Select**.

To import a TWAIN image

1 From the **File** menu, select **Import**, and then click **Acquire**.

2 Complete the procedure using the acquisition dialog associated with the selected TWAIN source.

3 The image will open in a new window.

Assuming the image is not in the native PhotoPlus (.SPP) format or the Adobe Photoshop (.PSD) format, it will contain a single layer, called **Background**.

Scanned images, especially colour, can be very large—in addition to using up your disk space, large files take a long time to load, save, and print. When scanning images, you should bear the following in mind:

For line art and halftone images

• If possible, scan at 600 dpi and (if saving) save as a black-and-white TIFF or PCX file.

For photographic images

• For colour images on a colour scanner, save as a colour TIFF file.

• For black-and-white photos, scan using greyscales and save as a greyscale TIFF.

> Note that the features available in image acquisition software vary widely and are not determined by PhotoPlus. Usually, you will at least be able to adjust settings for the image source (such as a colour photograph, black and white photograph, or colour halftone) and the resolution at which the image is to be scanned.
>
> For information on colour theory and tips on scanning images, see Chapter 8 of the *User Guide*.

Getting Images Into PhotoPlus

Working with open images

Once you have opened your images in the workspace, PhotoPlus provides various ways for you to work with and manipulate them. Of particular note are the new **Documents** tab thumbnail gallery and the **Zoom** and **Pan** tool image comparison features.

Using the Documents tab

Every time you open a file, PhotoPlus automatically adds a corresponding thumbnail to the **Documents** tab at the lower edge of the workspace. The **Documents** tab displays a thumbnail gallery of all your open image files and provides a quick and easy way to view and switch between images in the workspace.

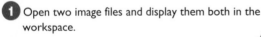

To switch between images

- On the **Documents** tab, simply click on the thumbnail of the image you want to view.

The image opens in the workspace.

Right-click a thumbnail in the **Documents** tab gallery to change the viewing options of an open image, for example, to close, minimize, or restore it.

To change image viewing options

- On the **Documents** tab, right-click a thumbnail and then click the desired option.

Comparing image files

With PhotoPlus, comparing images has never been easier! You can now zoom and pan multiple image windows simultaneously—particularly useful when you want to work on or compare detailed areas of two or more images.

To zoom into and out of multiple images

1. Open two image files and display them both in the workspace.

2. On the Standard toolbar, click the **Zoom** tool, then on the View context toolbar, select the **Zoom All Windows** option.

3 Left click on an image to zoom into both images.

- or-

Right click on an image to zoom out of both images.

To pan multiple images

1 Open two image files in the workspace.

2 Zoom into both images (see previous section), or make the image windows smaller, so that scrollbars display at the lower and right edges of both windows.

3 On the Standard toolbar, click the Pan tool, then on the View context toolbar, select the **Scroll All Windows** option.

4 Click and drag on one of the images. Notice that both image windows scroll simultaneously.

You'll find these comparison feature particularly useful for comparing multiple versions of the same image—for example to compare the effects of different lighting and contrast effects on a particular area of an image.

That concludes this tutorial. You now know how to browse and open images in PhotoPlus, and how to manipulate and compare open images using the Zoom and Pan tools. For step-by-step instructions on cropping, sharpening, making basic image corrections, and printing, continue working through the other tutorials in the **Getting Started** sequence.

Changing Image and Canvas Size

Once you've got your image into PhotoPlus, you can change the image size and/or the canvas size.

In this tutorial you'll learn how to:

- Adjust image size using the Image Size dialog.

- Scale and resample images.

- Use the Crop tool and Crop to Selection command.

- Create a balanced composition when cropping using the Rule of Thirds grid.

- Adjust canvas size using the Canvas Size dialog.

Changing Image and Canvas Size

Let's begin by explaining the difference between changing image size and changing canvas size in PhotoPlus.

- When you change **image size** (right), you are scaling the whole image (or selected region) up or down.

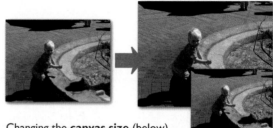

Image distortion

When you **resize an image**, you are in fact distorting it. This is because the image content is stretched or squashed. However, especially when downsizing, the distortion is subtle because PhotoPlus does a good job of **resampling** the image—that is, recalculating how to distribute the image pixels.

When you **resize the canvas**, the image pixels are undisturbed so there's no distortion.

- Changing the **canvas size** (below), simply involves adding or taking away pixels around the edges of the image. It's like adding to the neutral border around a mounted photo, or using scissors to crop the photo to a smaller size.

Changing image size

In this section, we'll use the **Image Size** dialog to specify a new size for our image.

To resize an entire image

1 Launch PhotoPlus and open any image file.

2 On the **Image** menu, click **Image Size**.

3 In the **Image Size** dialog:

- To link the screen dimensions (**Pixel Size**) to the printed dimensions (**Print Size**) settings, leave the **Resize layers** check box selected.

  To specify just the printed dimensions, clear the **Resize layers** check box.

- To retain the current image proportions, leave the **Maintain aspect ratio** check box selected.

  To alter the dimensions independently, clear the **Maintain aspect ratio** box.

Changing Image and Canvas Size

4 To adjust screen dimensions:

- In the **Pixel Size** section, select **pixels** or **percent** and then enter your new **Width** and/or **Height** value.

  Note that when you change one or both values, the corresponding values in the **Print Size** section automatically update.

  If you select the **Maintain aspect ratio box** (see step 3), when you change the width, the height updates correspondingly and vice versa.

  (If you clear the **Resize layers** box, you will not be able to change values in the **Pixel Size** section.)

- In the **Resampling method** section, drag the slider to select a resampling method.

To adjust printed dimensions:

- In the **Print Size** section, select your units of measurement and enter **Width** and/or **Height** values.

  If you select the **Maintain aspect ratio** option (see step 3), when you change the width, the height updates correspondingly and vice versa.

  If you select the **Resize layers** box, when you change one or both values, the corresponding values in the **Pixel Size** section automatically update.

  If you clear the **Resize layers** box, **Width** and **Height** values in the **Pixel Size** section are not affected.

- Enter your required image resolution.

- Drag the **Resampling method** slider to select a resampling method.

5 Click **OK**.

🔮 Choosing image resolution

The resolution you choose depends on what you want to do with the image.

For images that will be professionally printed, choose 300 pixels/inch (dpi).

For images that will be printed on a home printer, 150 to 200 dpi will usually be sufficient.

For images that will be viewed on-screen, choose 96 dpi—standard screen resolution.

Note that the higher the resolution the larger the resulting file size.

🔮 Choosing a resampling method

PhotoPlus provides a selection of resampling methods. Which one you choose depends on the content of the image, and how you want to resize it. As a rule:

Use **Nearest pixel** for hard-edge images.

Use **Bilinear interpolation** when shrinking photos.

Use **Bicubic interpolation** when enlarging photos.

Use **Lanczos3 Window** for best quality.

Changing Image and Canvas Size

Changing canvas size

PhotoPlus provides several ways of changing the canvas size:

- To simply reduce the canvas area, you can use the **Crop** tool or the **Crop to Selection** command.

- To either enlarge or reduce the canvas area, use the **Canvas Size** dialog to specify where pixels should be added or subtracted.

Using the Crop tool

When you crop an image, PhotoPlus deletes all of the pixels outside the crop selection area, and resizes the image canvas so that only the area inside the crop selection remains. As well as changing canvas size, you can use the **Crop** tool to remove unwanted parts of an image or to bring an area of an image into focus.

There are a number of ways to use the **Crop** tool in PhotoPlus. You can:

- Use the tool's basic functionality, defining the crop selection size yourself.

- Crop to a pre-defined print size.

- Use the **Rule of Thirds** grid option to aid in photo composition when cropping.

To crop the image with Crop tool

1 Open any image in the PhotoPlus workspace.

2 On the Tools toolbar, select the 🖾 **Crop** tool.

3 Drag out a rectangular crop selection area on the image.

(To constrain the region to a square, hold down the **Ctrl** key while dragging.)

4 If required, click and drag inside the selection to move the whole crop area (the cursor changes to the ✛ Move cursor), or drag the sizing handles.

5 Double-click inside the crop selection to crop to the designated size, or click ✔ on the Context toolbar.

Changing Image and Canvas Size

To crop to a pre-defined print size

1 Open any image in the PhotoPlus workspace.

2 On the Tools toolbar, select the 🔲 **Crop** tool.

3 On the Crop context toolbar, in the left-most drop-down list, choose a pre-defined print size. We chose 4 x 6 in.

4 Drag out to define your crop selection area.

5 Double-click inside the crop selection to crop to the designated size.

The print resolution adjusts to honour the print dimensions.

> 🚩 **Custom print sizes**
>
> You can also define a custom print size using the **Width** and **Height** boxes on the Crop context toolbar.

| Custom ▼ | 4.00 ▸ x 8.00 ▸ | inches ▼ |

To use the Rule of Thirds grid

1 On the Tools toolbar, select the 🔲 **Crop** tool.

2 On the Crop context toolbar:

- Select the **Thirds grid** check box.
- Choose a pre-defined, **Custom**, or **Unconstrained** crop selection area.

| Custom ▼ | 4.00 ▸ x 8.00 ▸ | inches ▼ | ☑ Shading ■ Opacity: 50 ▸ % ☑ Thirds grid ✓ ✗ |

3 Drag to define your crop area. A 3 x 3 grid is superimposed on your image.

4 For best results, position the subject of the photo at any of the four intersection points on the grid.

5 Double-click inside the crop selection to crop to the outer grid dimensions.

Changing Image and Canvas Size

To crop to selection

1 On the Tools toolbar, expand the ▢▾ Selection tools flyout and choose any of the Selection tools. We chose the **Ellipse Selection** tool.

2 Drag to define a crop selection area.

3 If required, click and drag inside the selection to reposition the crop area (the cursor changes to the ✛ Move cursor).

4 On the **Image** menu, click **Crop to Selection**.

Using the Canvas Size dialog

You can use the **Canvas Size** dialog to reduce or increase the canvas size by adding or subtracting pixels from the canvas border.

> 🔌 Cropping with the **Crop** tool or **Crop to Selection** command affects all image layers. This means that everything outside the selected crop area is eliminated.

To reduce the canvas size

1 On the **Image** menu, click **Choose Canvas Size**.

2 In the **Canvas Size** dialog:

- Select the required unit of measurement from the drop-down list box.
- Enter the required **New Width** and/or **New Height** values.

The **Current** canvas dimensions are shown for comparison.

In our example, we are reducing our 800 x 600 pixel canvas size to 75% of its original size.

> 🔌 Alternatively, select the **Relative** check box, and then simply enter the number of units you want to **subtract from** the existing width and height values—for example, 5 pixels, 1 cm, 10 percent, and so on.

Changing Image and Canvas Size

3 In the **Anchor** box, click to position the image thumbnail with respect to the edge(s) from where you want PhotoPlus to subtract pixels.

By default, PhotoPlus subtracts pixels equally from all sides of the image—so the centre anchor point is selected. But there may be times when you want to subtract pixels with respect to a particular edge. For example, to subtract pixels from the top of the canvas, click the lower anchor point, as illustrated.

4 Click **OK** to apply your changes.

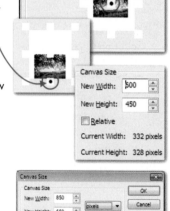

If you open the **Canvas Size** dialog again, you'll now see that the **width and height** values now reflect your new reduced canvas size.

To increase the canvas size

1 On the **Image** menu, click **Choose Canvas Size**.

2 In the **Canvas Size** dialog:

- Select the required unit of measurement from the drop-down list box.

- Enter the required **New Width** and/or **New Height** values (we are increasing our 800 x 600 pixel canvas size to 850 x 650 pixels).

3 In the **Anchor** box, click to position the image thumbnail with respect to the edge(s) to which you want PhotoPlus to add pixels (see previous).

> Alternatively, select the **Relative** check box, and enter the number of units you want to **add to** the existing width and height values.

4 Click **OK**.

The new canvas area is filled (on the **Background** layer) with the current background colour and (on standard layers) with transparency.

Changing Image and Canvas Size

Congratulations, you've reached the end of this tutorial! We hope you've found it useful and are now feeling more familiar with the various image and canvas resizing options offered in PhotoPlus.

You'll find more detailed information on some of the topics covered here—for example, image resolution and resampling—in the *PhotoPlus User Guide* and in online Help.

In the next tutorial, we'll show you how to make some basic image corrections, including fixing red eye, making brightness and contrast adjustments, and more.

Making Basic Image Corrections

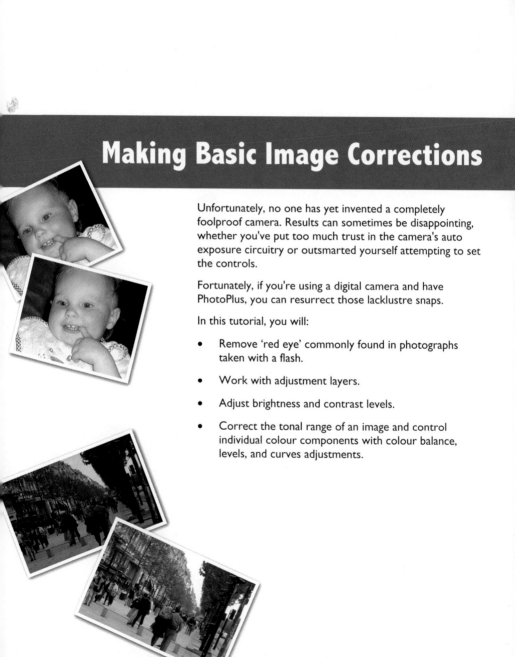

Unfortunately, no one has yet invented a completely foolproof camera. Results can sometimes be disappointing, whether you've put too much trust in the camera's auto exposure circuitry or outsmarted yourself attempting to set the controls.

Fortunately, if you're using a digital camera and have PhotoPlus, you can resurrect those lacklustre snaps.

In this tutorial, you will:

- Remove 'red eye' commonly found in photographs taken with a flash.

- Work with adjustment layers.

- Adjust brightness and contrast levels.

- Correct the tonal range of an image and control individual colour components with colour balance, levels, and curves adjustments.

Making Basic Image Corrections

Making Basic Image Adjustments

PhotoPlus provides a wealth of tools that allow you to correct, enhance, and manipulate your photographs. As you become more familiar—and more confident—with the photo-editing process, you'll no doubt want to experiment with all of these tools. If you're just starting out, however, it can be difficult to determine which particular tool or technique to use to best achieve the desired effect.

In this exercise, we'll introduce you to a selection of PhotoPlus tools and show you how to use them to correct some of the more common problems. You can make the adjustments to your own photographs, or you can use the sample images provided in your **Tutorials\Workspace** folder. In a default installation, you'll find this folder in the following location:

C:\Program Files\Serif\PhotoPlus\X2\Tutorials\Workspace

We'll begin by making a couple of adjustments to a close-up baby photograph. It doesn't take an expert eye to notice that this photo needs a red eye correction. In addition, the overall colour balance is a little too red. Let's get to work...

Correcting red eye

The **Red Eye** tool lets you correct the 'red eye' effect often seen in photos taken with a flash.

You can apply the tool to the active layer, or to a selected region on the active layer.

To use the Red Eye tool

1 Click **File**, then **Open**. Browse to locate your own image, or browse to the **Workspace** folder and open the **Red Eye.jpg** file.

2 On the Standard toolbar, click the 🔍 **Zoom** tool and then left-click to zoom in on the subject's pupil.

3 On the Tools toolbar, select the ◉ **Red Eye** tool.

4 Click and drag your mouse cursor over the eye, drawing an ellipse around the red eye area.

Don't make the ellipse too large as the tool may affect other red areas of the photograph.

5 Release the mouse button to correct the red eye problem.

6 Repeat to correct the other eye.

Making Basic Image Corrections

Great, we've fixed the first problem. Now let's do something about that colour balance.

Adjusting colour balance

The **Colour Balance** adjustment lets you adjust colour and tonal balance for general colour correction in the image.

You can apply this adjustment directly to your photograph, or as an adjustment layer. We'll use the latter method.

> **Adjustment layers**
>
> With the exception of red eye removal, we'll make all of our changes on adjustment layers. Adjustment layers let you insert any number of effects experimentally. Each adjustment layer applies one effect to content on the layers below it. You can even combine multiple effects by stacking several adjustment layers.
>
> Rather than altering the image directly (as with the **Image/Adjust** commands), adjustment layers let you revisit the settings for a given effect as often as needed. If you later decide you don't even need an effect, you can simply hide it or delete it! For more information, see "Using adjustment layers" in online Help.

To balance colour (using an adjustment layer)

1. At the bottom of the **Layers** tab, click the **New Adjustment Layer** button, then click **Colour Balance**.

   PhotoPlus adds a new **Colour Balance** adjustment layer to the **Layers** tab.

2. In the **Colour Balance** dialog:

   - In the **Tonal Balance** section, select **Shadows**, **Midtones**, or **Highlights** to determine which range of pixels in the image (dark, midrange, or bright) will be affected by the colour correction.

     We selected **Midtones**.

   - To keep the overall brightness of the image the same, select the **Preserve Lightness** check box.

3. In the **Colour Balance** section, drag one or more of the sliders to adjust colours along the **Cyan/Red**, **Magenta/Green**, and **Yellow/Blue** scales.

   In our example, we reduced the amount of magenta and the amount of red.

   Above the sliders, the corresponding **Colour Levels** boxes update to show the degree of adjustment.

Making Basic Image Corrections

4 To apply the adjustment, click **OK**.

- or -

To abandon changes, close the dialog, and remove the adjustment layer, click **Cancel**.

- or -

To reset the original colour balance, click **Reset**.

Our before and after images, right, show the difference that the colour balance adjustment has made to our photograph.

In the following sections, we'll use three different adjustment layers to correct the brightness and tonal range in an image.

Adjusting brightness and contrast

Brightness refers to the overall lightness or darkness, while contrast describes the tonal range, or spread between lightest and darkest values. The **Brightness/Contrast** adjustment is great if you want to quickly correct an image. You can apply the adjustment to the active layer, or to a selected region on the active layer.

To adjust brightness and contrast

1 Click **File**, then **Open**. Browse to the **Workspace** folder and open the **France.jpg** file (or use your own image).

2 On the **Layers** tab, click the 🖼 **New Adjustment Layer** button, then click **Brightness/Contrast**.

A new **Brightness/Contrast** adjustment layer is added to the **Layers** tab.

3 In the **Brightness/Contrast** dialog:

- Drag the **Brightness** slider to the right to increase the brightness percentage. (Or drag to the left to reduce brightness.)

- Drag the **Contrast** slider to the right to increase contrast; drag to the left to reduce contrast.

The active layer or selection updates each time you release the mouse button.

4 Click **OK** to apply the adjustment.

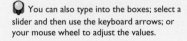
You can also type into the boxes; select a slider and then use the keyboard arrows; or your mouse wheel to adjust the values.

Making Basic Image Corrections

Our before and after images are shown right. We think you'll agree that there is a marked improvement.

Optional step: Quickly compare the adjusted image to the original by temporarily 'hiding' your adjustment level.

To do this, on the **Layers** tab, click the  **Hide/Show Layer** button for the **Brightness/Contrast** adjustment layer.

> To remove an adjustment layer (and its effect)
> On the **Layers** tab, simply select the adjustment layer you want to delete, and then click ⊠ **Delete Layer**.

Next, we'll adjust the tonal range of an image using a **Levels** adjustment layer.

Adjusting levels

The **Levels** dialog displays the proportion of image pixels at each lightness value, ranging from shadows through to highlights. By looking at the histogram, you can see if the image lacks a 'high end' or a 'low end,' or if too many pixels are clustered in the shadows.

To adjust tonal range using levels

1 Click **File**, then **Open**. Browse to the **Workspace** folder and open **Squirrel.png**.

2 On the **Layers** tab, click ▣ **New Adjustment Layer**, then click **Levels**.

In the **Levels** dialog, at the lower edge of the histogram, three sliders set the values displayed in the **Input** and **Gamma** boxes.

The left slider is set at **0** (pure black), the right slider at **255** (pure white). The middle slider adjusts the midtones of the image, effectively altering the overall brightness—move the slider to the left to increase brightness; move it to the right to decrease brightness.

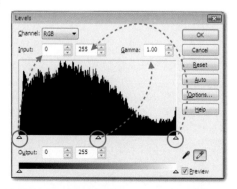

Making Basic Image Corrections

3 This histogram shows that our image lacks both a low (dark) end and a high (light) end. To correct this, drag the sliders to the edges of the group of pixels on either end of the histogram.

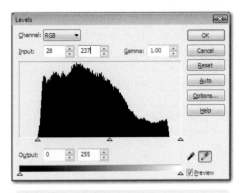

For example, if you move the left (black) slider to the right to level 28, PhotoPlus maps all the pixels at level 28 and lower to level 0. Similarly, if you move the right (white) slider to the left to level 237, PhotoPlus maps all pixels at level 237 and higher to level 255.

All of the pixels in the image are remapped and adjusted proportionately to maintain the overall colour balance.

💡 For more detailed information about adjusting levels and the **Levels** dialog, see the "Levels and Curves adjustments" topic in online Help.

As you adjust the sliders, your image updates in the workspace (provided you have not cleared the **Preview** check box in the lower right corner).

4 When you're happy with the results, click **OK**.

🔋 PhotoPlus also provides **Auto Levels**, which automatically adjusts the black and white points in an image. However, since this individually adjusts each colour channel, colour casts may be introduced.

We'll conclude this tutorial by using the **Curves** filter to adjust colour levels in an image. We'll apply this effect to the squirrel photo we used in the previous section. If we again use an adjustment layer, we can compare the individual effects of the **Levels** and **Curves** adjustments with the combined effect of both of these effects—simply by clicking the appropriate **Hide/Show Layer** buttons on the **Layers** tab.

Making Basic Image Corrections

Adjusting curves

Like the **Levels** adjustment (see previous section), the **Curves** adjustment lets you correct the tonal range of an image—the spread of lightness values through shadow, midtone, and highlight regions—and control individual colour components.

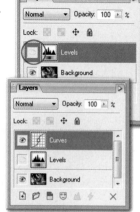

We'll start by hiding the **Levels** adjustment layer created in the previous exercise.

1 On the **Layers** tab:

- Click the ⬚ **Hide/Show Layer** button to hide the **Levels** adjustment layer.

- Click the ⬚ **New Adjustment Layer** button, then click **Curves**.

A **Curves** adjustment layer is added to the **Layers** tab and the **Curves** dialog opens.

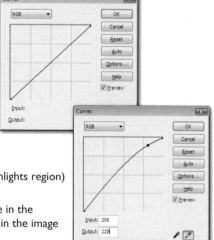

In the dialog, the tonal range of the photograph is shown initially as a straight, sloping line representing a 'before adjustment' spread of lightness values, from low to high.

By bending the line slightly at various points, you can shift those pixels to new values (lighter or darker), so the resulting 'after adjustment' curve produces a corrected image. In general, dragging the line down has a darkening effect; dragging it up has a lightening effect.

2 Click the upper section of the line (the highlights region) and drag it up and left, as illustrated right.

As you drag, PhotoPlus updates your image in the workspace. Notice that the highlight areas in the image have become slightly brighter.

3 When you're happy with your adjustment, click **OK**.

Making Basic Image Corrections

Now let's see what happens when we apply both the **Levels** and the **Curves** adjustments to our image...

4 On the **Layers** tab, click the  **Hide/Show Layer** button to once again display the **Levels** adjustment layer.

Our image is now brighter and displays more contrast—a subtle, but definite improvement over the original.

In this tutorial, we've demonstrated some of the fundamental image correction and adjustment tools provided in PhotoPlus.

If you've worked through the steps provided, you should now have a better understanding of the tools and techniques required to improve the quality of your digital images—or ultimately rescue the more unfortunate photographs from your Recycle Bin.

When you apply multiple adjustment layers to an image, you may need to go back and fine-tune each layer to achieve the best overall result.

Sharpening Images

No matter how experienced a photographer you are, there will be times when you'll want to 'sharpen' a photograph. For example, if you use a desktop scanner, you'll often find that your scanned images are slightly blurry.

In this tutorial, we'll discuss the various sharpening tools provided in PhotoPlus, and explain how and when to apply them.

You'll learn how to:

- Apply Sharpen, Sharpen More, and Sharpen Edges effects.

- Apply an Unsharp Mask filter.

- Adjust Unsharp Mask settings to suit image properties.

- Choose Unsharp Mask settings appropriate for screen and printed images.

- Use the Sharpen tool to increase the contrast in an area of an image.

Sharpening Images

Sharpening is an important step in digital photo editing, but it can be difficult to achieve the optimum results. PhotoPlus provides several different methods for sharpening your images; the tool and settings you use depend on the effect you want to achieve, and what you intend to do with your final image.

We'll apply various sharpening methods to the same photograph so that you can compare the result achieved by each method. You'll find our sample image, **Picnic.jpg** in your **Workspace** folder. In a standard installation, this is installed to the following location:

C:\Program Files\Serif\PhotoPlus\X2\Tutorials\Workspace

Sharpen and Sharpen More

The **Sharpen** and **Sharpen More** effects enhance differences between adjacent pixels of different colours. Both of these effects apply varying degrees of sharpening to an entire image, with a single click.

Note that while these effects are quick and simple to use, they don't offer the control of some of the other methods discussed later in this tutorial.

To apply the Sharpen effect

- On the **Effects** menu, choose **Sharpen**, then select **Sharpen** from the submenu.

original   Sharpen

As you can see, a subtle sharpening effect has been applied to the original image. The effect has particularly enhanced sharpness in the subjects' faces, in the grass, and in the basket of flowers. The image is slightly sharper, but stills maintains its 'softness.'

- On the **Edit** menu, select **Undo Sharpen** (or press **Ctrl+Z**) to revert to your original image.

Let's now see what happens when we apply the **Sharpen More** effect.

To apply the Sharpen More effect

- On the **Effects** menu, choose **Sharpen**, then select **Sharpen More**.

Sharpening Images

original

Sharpen More

The sharpening effect here is much more aggressive and less successful—the faces, flowers, and the blades of grass are overly defined and the overall smoothness of the image is lost.

- Press **Ctrl+Z** to revert to your original image.

Sharpen Edges

The **Sharpen Edges** effect also works without a dialog, this time applying sharpening only to edges while still preserving the overall smoothness of the image.

To apply the Sharpen Edges effect

- On the **Effects** menu, choose **Sharpen**, then select **Sharpen Edges**.

original

Sharpen Edges

Just as you would expect, applying this effect has produced a more subtle effect. Edges and lines are crisper, but the image remains smooth.

- Press **Ctrl+Z** to revert to your original image.

Sharpening Images

Unsharp Mask

Unsharp Mask works mainly to enhance the edges in an image. Unlike **Sharpen Edges**, however, this effect is applied through a dialog so you have ultimate control over the various settings.

While the **Sharpen** and **Sharpen More** effects are often adequate for enhancing sharpness in graphics, the **Unsharp Mask** filter is generally considered to be the standard tool for adjusting sharpness in photographs. It is excellent for improving image quality, especially with scanned or resized pictures. You can apply this correction on a **filter layer** (recommended), or directly to your image.

To apply an Unsharp Mask effect on a filter layer

1 On the **Layers** tab, right-click the layer you want to sharpen and click **Convert to Filter Layer**.

2 In the **Filter Gallery**, expand the **Sharpen** category and click the **Unsharp Mask** thumbnail swatch.

- To see a different part of the image, drag with the hand cursor.

- In the drop-down list, select a different magnification if required.

3 In the right pane, adjust the effect by dragging the **Amount**, **Radius**, and **Threshold** sliders, or by typing values directly into the value boxes.

- **Amount** controls the degree of sharpening at an edge (how much darker/lighter the edge borders become). This setting has a large effect on the image. Values between 80 and 120 are common.

- **Radius** determines the spread of pixels (surrounding an edge) that will be affected. A radius value of 1 is generally a good starting point, with values between 0.6 and 2 also being useful.

  For fine detail and/or low resolution images, use a lower radius setting (to avoid obliterating detail). Use higher settings with higher resolution images, where pixels are smaller relative to image elements.

> Filter layers let you add effects experimentally. You can turn them on and off to compare 'before' and 'after' images by clicking the layer's 👁 **Hide/Show** icon.
>
> You can also edit or delete the effect later—simply double-click the filter layer to reopen the **Filter Gallery** and make your changes as required.

> You can also adjust the **Amount**, **Radius**, and **Threshold** sliders by using your keyboard arrow keys or your mouse wheel.

> **Radius** and **Amount** interact—reducing one value allows for an increase in the other.

Screen and print settings

Bear in mind that images need different adjustments depending on how they are going to be viewed—on screen or in print. More radius is required for higher resolution images intended for print, less radius for lower resolution images that will be viewed on screen.

- **Threshold** sets the degree of colour difference required across an edge before the effect is applied. Set this value too high and you'll see very little change in your image. Generally, values between 0 and 5 are useful. Use a higher threshold for grainy images or skin tones (5 or sometimes more), so the filter won't merely amplify noise in the image.

In our example, we used the following values:

Amount—120; **Radius**—1; **Threshold**—5

original   Unsharp Mask

As you can see, applying an **Unsharp Mask** effect to this image has produced a subtle, yet very effective result. The subjects' faces are enhanced, and detail in the flowers and background is revealed, without introducing 'noise' or other artefacts.

- Press **Ctrl+Z** to revert to your original image.

 Getting creative

In our example, our aim was to achieve a subtle sharpening effect to enhance our photograph.

However, don't forget that sharpening can also be a creative tool. Sometimes you might want to make an image much sharper than it really is, to tell a story, make a point, emphasize an area of interest, or create an interesting visual effect.

Sharpening Images

Sharpen tool

The previous methods we've discussed allow you to increase the sharpness of an entire image. But what if you only want to sharpen certain areas of an image? PhotoPlus has a tool just for this purpose!

The **Sharpen** tool lets you enhance apparent sharpness in an area of an image by increasing contrast under the brush.

To use the Sharpen tool

1 On the Tools toolbar, on the Retouch Tools flyout, select the ▣ **Sharpen** tool.

2 On the **Brush Tip** tab, select a brush tip style and size.

3 If required, adjust **Size**, **Blend Mode**, and **Opacity** on the Brush context toolbar.

before

4 Click (or drag for large areas) to sharpen the image under the brush.

In our example, we've used the **Sharpen** tool to increase sharpness in the flowers.

after

Well done, you've now experimented with the various sharpening methods provided in PhotoPlus. We hope that you're feeling more confident with the tools and techniques discussed here, and are ready to work on some of your own images.

Some general tips to keep in mind:

- For optimum sharpening of an entire photograph, use the **Unsharp Mask** filter and experiment with different settings until you achieve the desired results.

- When choosing sharpening settings, don't forget to consider your image resolution and output (print or screen). In general, use a higher **Radius** setting for higher resolution images intended for print, less radius for lower resolution images that will be viewed on screen.

- When using the **Sharpen** tool to bring out fine detail in an area of an image, choose a small brush tip and click in the area rather than dragging across it. In general, less is more, so don't overdo it or you'll add unwanted 'noise' and artefacts to the image.

Printing Photographs

You've cropped your photographs, sharpened them, and made all the necessary image adjustments. All the hard work is done and you're now ready to print out your images and share them with family and friends.

PhotoPlus provides you with a range of printing options. In this tutorial, we'll step you through the basic printing process and show you how to set up options for printing professionally or from your desktop printer.

You'll learn how to:

- Quickly print a single image to a sheet of paper.

- Resize and reposition your image on the printed page.

- Set professional printing options—colour separations, file information, and printer marks.

- Print multiple images using a layout template.

- Print multiple images using a custom layout.

Printing Photographs

Before you begin the printing process, you need to decide how you want to print your image(s). You may simply want to print from your own desktop printer, if so, PhotoPlus has everything you need to print single or multiple images in various layouts. However, if you intend to use a professional printer, PhotoPlus supports additional options—colour separations, printer marks, etc—to help you get the best possible results.

To begin, we'll step you through the process of printing from a desktop printer and show you how to change print settings. We'll then discuss setting up options for a professional printing job. Finally, we'll demonstrate the **Print Multiple** option, which allows you to print multiple images (or copies of an image) on the same sheet.

Desktop printing

This first section assumes that you want to quickly print a single image from your printer.

To quickly print a single photo or image

1 Open the image in the PhotoPlus workspace.

2 On the Standard toolbar, click the 🖻 **Print** button, or on the **File** menu, click **Print**.

In the **Print** dialog, on the **General**

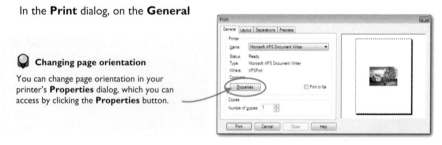

> 💡 **Changing page orientation**
>
> You can change page orientation in your printer's **Properties** dialog, which you can access by clicking the **Properties** button.

tab, the **Preview** area on the right shows where on the page the image will be printed. This changes according to whether the printer driver is set to portrait (tall) or landscape (wide) orientation.

3 On the **General** tab, select your printer and the number of copies you want to print. If necessary, click the **Properties** button to set up your printer—for example, to determine the correct page size, printer tray, paper type, and so on.

4 Optional step: Click the other tabs to set special print options (see next sections).

5 Click **Print**.

The image is printed in colour on a colour printer or in shades of grey on a black and white printer.

> ⬇ The printed size depends on the dimensions you've specified in the **Image Size** dialog (accessed from the **Image** menu). For details, see the "Changing Image and Canvas Size" tutorial or online Help.

To set print options (before you print)

1 In the **Print** dialog, click the **Layout** tab.

2 On the **Layout** tab:

- To specify the absolute position of the top left corner of the image, clear the **Centre Image** check box and then enter the new **Left** and **Top** position values.

  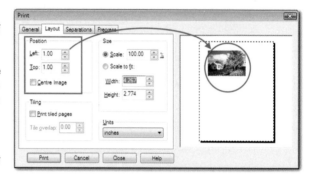

  PhotoPlus displays the new position of the image in the right Preview pane.

- To print at actual size, select **Scale** and choose **100%**.

  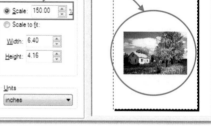

- To print at a larger or smaller size, choose or type a different percentage value in the list.

- PhotoPlus displays the new image size in the right Preview pane.

- To resize your image to fill the whole page, select the **Scale to fit** option.

- To specify exact dimensions, enter a value in either the **Width** or **Height** box.

  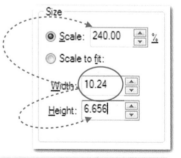

  PhotoPlus maintains the aspect ratio of the image and automatically calculates the corresponding **Width** or **Height**, and **Scale** percentage values.

If you want to significantly increase the size of your image, we suggest that you do this in the **Image Size** dialog, prior to printing. For step-by-step instructions, see the "Changing Image and Canvas Size" tutorial.

While you can use the **Print** dialog to scale an image, you risk losing image resolution if you increase your image size using this method.

Printing Photographs

- To print oversized artwork on several sheets of paper, select the **Print tiled pages** check box.

  Use this option to print at sizes larger than the maximum paper size of your printer (for banners or posters, etc).

  Each 'tile' is printed on a single sheet of paper, which you can then join to form a complete page.

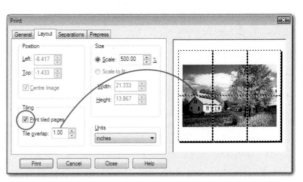

To simplify arrangement of the tiles and to allow for printer margins, you can also specify a **Tile overlap** value.

3 When you've made all of your required layout changes, click **Print**.

Professional printing

The **Print** dialog also contains the **Separations** and **Prepress** tabs, which contain advanced options for professional printing. If all your printing requirements are met by your desktop printer, you probably won't need to use these tabs; however, you might still find it useful to understand a little about what they offer.

To set print options for professional printing

If you're printing with **CMYK process colour**, you can use the **Separations** tab to print colour separations.

1 In the **Print** dialog, click the **Separations** tab.

Normally, process colour output gives you four sheets or **separations** per publication page: one each for the Cyan, Magenta, Yellow, and blacK (CMYK) ink components in the image. Only these separations will be printed.

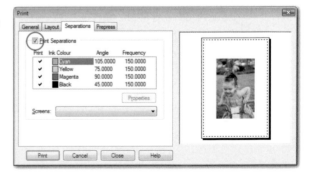

2 Select the **Print Separations** check box to specify that colour separations are to be printed.

3 To select or deselect a colour separation, click on its corresponding check box.

An offset printing press needs one independent plate for each colour that will print. PhotoPlus lets you print the colour separations that are used when printing the job to an image-setter—that is, for each page, you will get one complete negative for each of the four colours.

This option is only available if the currently selected Windows printer is a PostScript® printer. When outputting as PostScript, select the **Print to file** check box on the **General** tab prior to printing.

4 In the **Screens** drop-down list, select a screen appropriate to the paper type you'll be using.

- or -

Choose **Custom** and then click the **Properties** button to define a custom screen.

5 To specify the file information and printer marks you want to include, click the **Prepress** tab.

6 In the **Printer Marks** section, select the appropriate check boxes to include file information and/or printer marks on your printout.

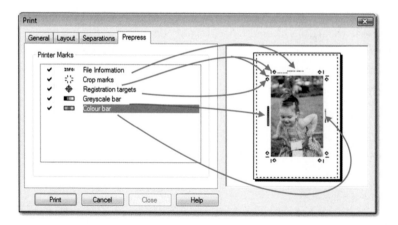

To ensure that the file information and printer marks are entirely visible on the final print, the printer page size must be at least 1" x 1" larger than the actual artwork being printed.

For PostScript printing, the Windows printer driver normally has some 'extra' page sizes, which can be used with standard artwork paper sizes.

Printing Photographs

Printing multiple images

PhotoPlus lets you make the most of expensive photo-quality printing paper by arranging several images onto a single output sheet. Simply choose a layout template (or design your own), then drag and drop open images into the cells on the preview page. Once you've placed images into a layout, you can move, resize, rotate, or flip them—and of course, print out your page!

To print one or more images using a layout template

1 On the **File** menu, choose **Print Multiple**.

The PhotoPlus window displays:

- At the top—a toolbar providing useful command buttons. For example, you can open other images; save your layout; set up print options; hide or display the dot grid; turn off snapping; stretch, scale, and rotate your placed images, and so on.

- To the left—a scrolling thumbnail gallery of your currently open images.

- In the centre—a page layout region.

- To the right—a drop-down list and scrolling gallery of layout templates.

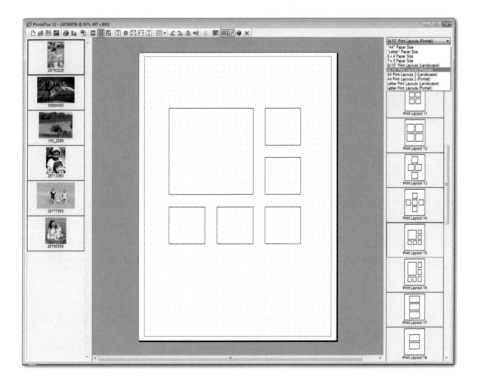

Printing Photographs

2 To open additional images for printing, click the 🖼 **Open Images** button.

A new thumbnail displays for each image opened.

> 🛈 Note that any additional images opened while in Print Multiple mode will be closed when you return to the main workspace.

3 In the upper right drop-down list, select a template size and orientation (we chose **A4 Print Layouts 2 (Portrait)**. Then, in the scrolling gallery, click on a template to display it in the page layout region (we chose **Print Layout 15**).

4 On the toolbar, click the 🖽 **Preferences** button.

5 In the **Preferences** dialog, on the **General** tab, select a fit method to determine how images scale into the template layout cells.

The following fit methods are available:

- **Scale to Fit (default):** Fits into the cell with no cropping, distortion, or rotation.
- **Stretch to Fit:** Fills the cell completely, with no rotation.
- **Rotate/Scale to Fit:** Rotates or scales to fit the cell, with no cropping or distortion.
- **Fit Width:** Fills across the width of the cell, cropping height if necessary.
- **Fit Height:** Fills the height of the cell, cropping width if necessary.

Scale to Fit

Stretch to Fit

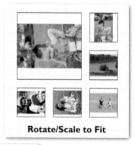

Rotate/Scale to Fit

Fit Width

Fit Height

Printing Photographs

6 On the **Layout** tab, if required, you can:

- In the **Rulers/Grid** section—set the Print Multiple dot grid measurement units.

- In the **Grid Spacing** section—set the horizontal and vertical grid spacing.

- In the **Grid Colour** section—click the colour swatch to change the colour of the dot grid.

  This opens the **Adjust Colour** dialog. Simply click in the colour wheel to define a new colour.

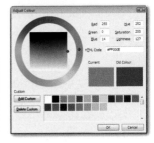

> The **Layout** tab settings are independent of the main PhotoPlus layout preferences.

7 When you are happy with your settings, click **OK** to close the **Preferences** dialog.

8 Drag and drop your image thumbnails directly onto the template cells.

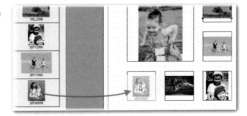

9 To change the position of an individual image with respect to its cell borders, simply select the image and then click one of the following toolbar buttons:

- **Scale to Fit**
- **Stretch to Fit**
- **Rotate/Scale to Fit**
- **Fit Width**
- **Fit Height**
- **Align** flyout

10 When all your images are placed, click the **Print** button to open the **Print** dialog (see "To set print options," previous).

11 Click **X** **Close** to return to the main PhotoPlus workspace.

While PhotoPlus provides a wide selection of print templates from which to choose, there may be times when you want to create your own layout. You can do this by switching from the default ▦ **Automatic Mode**—which uses the templates to determine the multi-image layout, to 🔲 **Manual Mode**, which allows you to freely move and resize your images on the page layout. Let's do this now.

To print one or more images using a custom layout

1 On the Print Multiple toolbar, click the 🔲 **Manual Mode** button.

The template cell outlines (and the template gallery itself) disappear, leaving an empty page and the current images displayed in the thumbnail gallery.

2 Drag an image onto the page, then drag into the desired position, or use the **Status Editor** dialog for precise placement.

💡 You can also use the arrow keys on your keyboard to 'nudge' a selected image into place.

3 You can save your layout at any point by clicking the 💾 **Save Layout** button.

Optional step: If you want to create a template based on your custom layout, simply switch back to **Automatic Mode** (which restores cells around each image), then right-click in the template gallery and choose **Add Category.**

In the **Category** dialog, type a name for your new category and click **OK**.

Once you have added your own category, ensure it is the selected category in the template gallery, then right click in template gallery and choose **Add Template**.
In the **New Template** dialog, type a name for your new template and click **OK**.

Your template displays in the template gallery.

That concludes our tutorial on printing, and the **Getting Started** sequence. You should now be feeling much more at ease with the basic PhotoPlus workflow—from getting your images into the workspace, right through to printing them out. We hope you've enjoyed the exercises and are feeling well-equipped to see your own projects through from start to finish.

Basics

These exercises provide an introduction to foundation concepts and basic PhotoPlus features.

- **Key Concepts**
- **Selection Tools**
- **Colour Spaces**
- **Image Formats**
- **Brush Tips and Tricks**

Key Concepts

If you're new to photo-editing programs, this tutorial provides illustrated step-by-step instructions to help you get to grips with the fundamental points.

The following concepts are discussed:

- Cropping
- Image size and canvas size
- Interacting tools and tabs
- Selection tools
- Foreground and background colours
- Layers
- Opacity and transparency
- Saving and exporting

Key Concepts

PhotoPlus provides you with a wealth of powerful photo-editing tools. In fact, if you're a new user, you may be wondering where to start! In the following pages, we aim to introduce you to the basics and make your experience with PhotoPlus as productive and enjoyable as possible!

We also suggest that you browse the contents of the **How To** tab (located on the left of the workspace). Here, you'll find illustrated step-by-step instructions to help you achieve the most popular photo-editing tasks.

Cropping

There are many reasons you may want to crop an image, for example, to change the composition of a photograph or to select only a particular portion of the image to use in a design.

1️⃣ To start, click 🖉 **Open**, choose **File/Open...** or select **open saved work** from the Startup Wizard. Browse to your **Tutorials/Workspace** folder and open the **Wheel.jpg** file.

In a default installation, you'll find this in the following location:

C:\Program Files\Serif\PhotoPlus\X2\Tutorials\Workspace

2️⃣ On the **Image** menu, choose **Canvas Size.**

Type 400 in the **New Width** box and 300 in the **New Height** box.

Select the left corner as the anchor point and click **OK**.

We've just reduced the size of an image by cropping it so only the upper left corner remains, as illustrated.

Press **Ctrl+Z** to undo the canvas cropping.

> 💡 You've no doubt heard of pixels—the dots of 'paint' that comprise an image on your computer. This photograph happens to be 800 pixels wide by 532 pixels high. If you wanted to change these dimensions, there are two ways to go about it and that's where canvas size and image size come into play. By changing the canvas size, you add or remove pixels at the edges of the image—rather like adding a border around a mounted photograph or taking a pair of scissors and snipping the photo to a smaller size.

Resizing

Changing the image size, on the other hand, means scaling the whole image up or down.

3 Choose **Image Size...** from the **Image** menu.

Under **Pixel Size**, in the **Width** box, type **400**.

Click in the **Height** box and 266 appears. (Because the **Maintain aspect ratio** box is checked, the image will retain its original proportions.)

Click **OK**.

Again, we have a 400 pixel wide image, but this time the whole image is preserved!

Press **Ctrl+Z** to restore the original image.

For more information about cropping images, and changing image and canvas size, see the "Changing Image and Canvas Size" tutorial.

The following sections of this tutorial focus on another basic concept: the **interaction** between the various PhotoPlus **tools** and the **context toolbar**, which extends each tool's functionality.

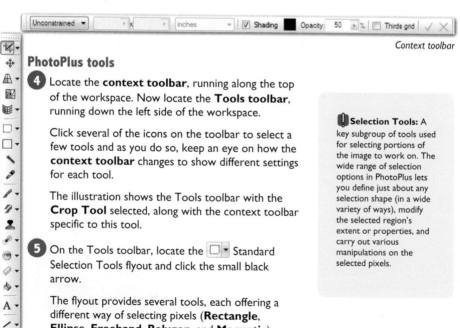

Context toolbar

PhotoPlus tools

4 Locate the **context toolbar**, running along the top of the workspace. Now locate the **Tools toolbar**, running down the left side of the workspace.

Click several of the icons on the toolbar to select a few tools and as you do so, keep an eye on how the **context toolbar** changes to show different settings for each tool.

The illustration shows the Tools toolbar with the **Crop Tool** selected, along with the context toolbar specific to this tool.

> **Selection Tools:** A key subgroup of tools used for selecting portions of the image to work on. The wide range of selection options in PhotoPlus lets you define just about any selection shape (in a wide variety of ways), modify the selected region's extent or properties, and carry out various manipulations on the selected pixels.

5 On the Tools toolbar, locate the ☐ Standard Selection Tools flyout and click the small black arrow.

The flyout provides several tools, each offering a different way of selecting pixels (**Rectangle**, **Ellipse**, **Freehand**, **Polygon**, and **Magnetic**).

Move the cursor across the icons and watch the HintLine at the bottom of the workspace. As for all PhotoPlus tools, you'll see condensed hints and tips on usage: in this case, keyboard shortcuts that enhance each tool.

Tools toolbar

Key Concepts

6 Choose the first tool from the submenu, the  **Rectangle Selection** tool. The context toolbar now shows a drop-down list which allows you to choose the type of selection you want to use: Normal, Fixed Size, Fixed Aspect, Rows, or Cols.

For example, **Fixed Size** creates a selection of the stated size, whereas **Rows** creates a selection encompassing only rows. For this tutorial, select **Normal**.

In the image, click in the sky slightly above the wheel just to the left of the centre. Drag down and right until you've drawn a selection bounding box—shown by a dashed line—down to the wheel's hub.

7 Click inside and drag slightly in any direction. As you can see, you can simply drag with any of the selection tools to adjust the position of the marquee. But what about the image inside the selection?

8 On the Tools toolbar, click the Move tool and use it to drag the selected region. This time, the image itself moves along with the marquee, as illustrated.

You'll notice it leaves behind a 'hole' in the image which brings us to our next concept: **foreground and background colours**. At any given time, PhotoPlus allows you to work with one of each.

Foreground and background colours

9 Locate and display the **Colour** tab (initially located on the right side of the workspace), and look for the two square colour swatches at the left.

The upper swatch represents the current foreground colour; the lower swatch the background colour.

Notice that the hole left by dragging the selection is filled with the background colour, in this case, white.

10 Press **Ctrl+Z** to return the selection to its original place. Now move the cursor over the 'rainbow' region of the **Colour** tab and you'll see the cursor change to a dropper icon.

Left-click anywhere in the spectrum and the foreground colour swatch changes; right-click anywhere else in the spectrum to change the background colour.

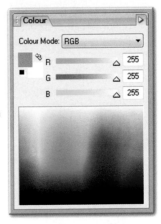

Layers

11 Drag the selection again. This time, the new background colour fills the hole. Press **Ctrl+Z** again and leave the region selected.

Locate and display the **Layers** tab; you should see one item in the list, labelled "Background."

On the **Layers** menu, choose **New Layer from Selection Copy**.

The main image doesn't appear to have changed—but it has, as the **Layers** tab confirms. There's now a brand new, transparent layer on top of the original (opaque) **Background** layer.

The concept of a vertical "stack" is a good way to think of **layers**, which provide an essential way of keeping different regions of an image separate from each other until it's time to stitch them back together into a single composite. The **Layers** tab lets you pick the layer you want to work on and create all kinds of magical interactions between layers. For more detailed information about layers, see the *PhotoPlus User Guide*.

12 On the **Layers** tab, right-click the **Background** layer and choose **Duplicate...**.

Click **OK** in the **Duplicate Layer** dialog and a copy of the original layer—called **Background Copy**—appears above the original in the **Layers** tab.

Still using the **Move** tool, drag the selection up into the sky—proof that it's separate from the **Background** layer!

Over on the **Layers** tab, click the small ▶ arrow next to **Opacity** and a small slider appears. Drag the slider to the halfway position and watch the selection respond.

Opacity and **transparency** are complementary, like "half full" and "half empty." They both refer to how much a particular pixel's colour contributes to the overall colour at that point in the image. Individual pixels can have opacity (which the Eraser tools, for example, can reduce). Just now, however, we changed the **Opacity** property of the whole layer—without actually changing the pixels. Whichever word you use, opacity or transparency is one of the cornerstones of digital painting: master this concept and great things will follow!

Key Concepts

Saving and exporting

Our final basic concept—**saving and exporting**—may sound trivial, but in fact it's one of the more subtle and helpful features of PhotoPlus.

You can save or export an image in the PhotoPlus .SPP format, or in another image format (.for example, .JPG or .GIF).

The .SPP format preserves all 'project' information you have added to image, such as multiple layers, masks, and paths. However, with the exception of .PSD format, all other image formats 'flattens' this data into a single layer, so you won't be able to edit it later.

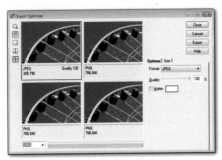

For exporting, PhotoPlus provides the versatile **Export Optimizer**, which provides a variety of options for each supported file format, and allows you to compare image quality using different settings and retain your preferred settings for each format. (See the "Image Formats" tutorial.)

Well, we certainly haven't produced any great art in this tutorial, but that was never the goal. Instead, we've touched briefly on some important concepts that might otherwise have escaped you. Hope it's been worthwhile!

Selection Tools

There are times in photo editing when you'll want to change the whole image at once. More often than not, however, you'll need to perform an operation on just part of the image.

The PhotoPlus selection tools provide a wide variety of ways to separate certain pixels from the others. In this tutorial, we'll cover the basic tools and techniques, along with properties that determine exactly what kind of selection you end up with.

You'll work with the following tools:

- ☐▾ Standard Selection tools
- ✎ Colour Selection tool
- Ⓐ Text Selection tool
- ☐▾ Adjustable Selection tools

Selection Tools

The techniques and tools demonstrated in this tutorial can be used on any of your own images. Alternatively, you can use the sample images provided in your **Tutorials\Workspace** folder.

In a standard installation, you'll find this folder in the following location:

C:\Program Files\Serif\PhotoPlus\X2\Tutorials\Workspace

1 Open PhotoPlus, and in the Startup Wizard select **create new picture**. (If PhotoPlus is already open, click 🗋 **New** to open the Startup Wizard.)

In the **New Image** dialog, accept the default settings and click **OK**.

2 On the Tools toolbar, click the **Paintbrush** tool. On the **Colour** tab, set the foreground colour of your choice.

3 On the **Brush Tip** tab, choose a large brush and then click and drag on your page to create a brush stroke.

4 On the Tools toolbar, click the 🔲▾ Standard Selection tools button to display the flyout.

Hover your cursor across the buttons to see the names of each selection tool—🔲 **Rectangle**, ⬭ **Ellipse**, ⟲ **Freehand**, ⟲ **Polygon**, and ⟲ **Magnetic**.

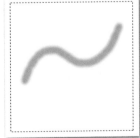

As you hover over the first four of these tools, the Hintline at the bottom of the workspace displays the following message:

"Drag out region, Ctrl-drag to constrain, +Shift to add, +Alt to subtract; after selecting, press Ctrl to move, Ctrl+Alt to duplicate."
Let's see if this is true!

4 Choose the 🔲 **Rectangle Selection** tool and drag a selection bounding box around the brush stroke. Try constraining the selection to a square by holding down the **Ctrl** key while dragging.

5 Release the mouse button; a selection bounding box appears (indicated by a moving dotted line).

You can move the box around using the ⬦ Move cursor.

Selection Tools

- If you now hold down the **Ctrl** key and drag the box, you move its contents (notice how the background colour is now exposed). Press **Ctrl+Z** to undo the move.

- Now press **Ctrl+Alt** and drag.

  This shortcut is incredibly handy—in fact, it's the only convenient way to copy and paste on the same layer. (You may want to undo the copy at this point, so as not to clutter up the screen.)

- Now try moving the brush stroke around your page using **Ctrl**-drag.

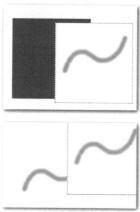

If you're working on a complex region, it's highly likely that you won't get the selection exactly right the first time. That's where adding and subtracting come in.

6 On the Tools toolbar, on the QuickShape flyout, select the **Rectangle**.

On the Context toolbar, click the **Fill Bitmap** button and then click and drag to draw a rectangle.

Optional step: To change the colour of your QuickShape, use the ◆ **Flood Fill** tool.

7 Click the **Rectangle Selection** tool again and select your rectangle.

- Now hold down the **Alt** key and select the lower right corner of the rectangle.

- Release the mouse button and you're left with a notched selection area.

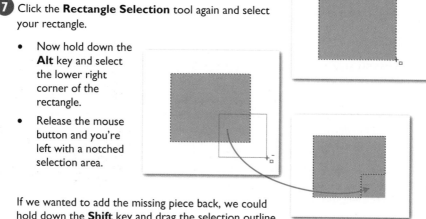

If we wanted to add the missing piece back, we could hold down the **Shift** key and drag the selection outline back to its original position. Instead of doing this, however, let's move on and look at the four Combination buttons located on the context toolbar:

▣ **New**, ▣ **Add**, ▣ **Subtract**, and ▣ **Intersect**.

Selection Tools

8 Click the 🔲 **Add** button and just drag—don't press any keys—from inside the selection bounding box to the rectangle's lower right corner. Now the whole shape should be selected again.

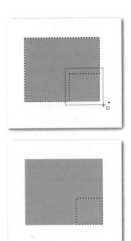

Three of the combination buttons duplicate the standard behaviour of the selection tool, that is, they save you the trouble of pressing **Shift** or **Alt**. However, **Intersect** is unique, with no key-assisted equivalent.

9 With the whole rectangle selected, click the **Intersect** button. Now select the lower right corner once again. This time, instead of a notched selection area (as in step 7), PhotoPlus leaves you with just the lower right corner selected.

Once you've seen the result:

- Click **Deselect** (or press **Ctrl+D**) to deselect everything.

- Save the file—we'll return to it later.

> 💧 You may also want to try the **Ellipse**, **Freehand**, and **Polygon** selection tools, applying the same add/subtract options.

There will be times when you'll want to outline something precisely. Let's see if we can do this using the **Freehand Selection** tool.

10 Click **File**, then **Open**. Browse to the **Tutorials\Workspace** folder and open the **Selection_3.jpg** file.

Click the 🔾 **Freehand Selection** tool and use it to trace the edges of the leaf. Unless you have a practiced hand and a drawing tablet, you'll be adding and subtracting all day!

Don't feel you need to finish the leaf outline. The **Freehand Selection** tool is useful for many selection needs, but PhotoPlus provides another tool that will make this particular job much easier...

11 Choose the 🖌 **Colour Selection Tool**. On the Context toolbar, set the **Tolerance** to **100** and select the **Contiguous** check box.

Now click in the middle of the leaf. How much time did you just save?

The leaf is an ideal candidate for the **Colour Selection** tool. It has rather uniform coloration in its region of interest, against a sharply contrasting surround.

12 Now undo your selection (**Ctrl+D**) and try clicking at various points using different **Tolerance** settings. You should see that different parts of the image become selected.

> If you click on a strong colour, then the selection tends to be restricted to that colour family. If you click in a region of higher lightness, there is some 'bleeding' into regions of comparable lightness. Did you get the same results?

13 On the Context toolbar, clear the **Contiguous** check box. Now click in the centre of the leaf once again.

Can you predict which portions of the image (those with similar coloration) will be selected?

PhotoPlus also provides the **Text Selection** tool, which you can use to create a selection in the form of text.

14 Close the **Selection_3.jpg** file and return to the file containing your rectangle QuickShape.

15 Choose the ⬚ **Rectangle Selection** tool and on the Context toolbar, set the **Feather** property to 10 pixels.

16 Drag to select a region (about 70 pixels x 70 pixels) over a white portion of the image. The selection box will appear larger than the dragged-out region (we'll explain why in a moment).

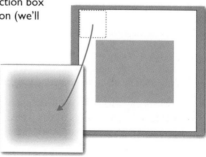

17 On the **Select** menu, click **Paint to Select**.

Paint to Select mode lets you see the original image as if through an overlay where any selected regions are coloured in red (using the default settings, which you can alter by clicking **Select**, then **Paint to Select Options**).

The colour's intensity varies depending on the level of selection of underlying pixels. Feathering, as you can see, has extended the selection 10 pixels in each direction, with the feathered edges tapering off to a lesser selection.

Selection Tools

On the **Colour** tab, also notice that the **Colour Mode** has switched to **Greyscale** with white as the foreground colour. That's so you can paint, erase, and use other tools directly on the overlay to alter the selected region.

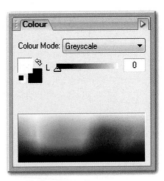

- Painting in white creates a 100% selection.
- Painting in black decreases the level of selection.
- Painting in grey creates a partial selection.

18 Click the ✏ **Paintbrush** tool.

Scribble anywhere on the overlay, just to see the result; the red line represents the level of selection.

19 Now click the double arrow on the **Colour** tab to switch the foreground colour to black.

20 On the **Brush Tip** tab, choose the 32-pixel soft brush. Click once in the centre of the selected (red) region and you'll create a deselected 'hole' with fuzzy edges.

21 Now return to standard mode—on the **Select** menu, click to clear **Paint to Select**.

Any region that's selected to any degree will be inside the selection bounding box We know for a fact that some of those 'inside pixels are only partially selected.

To demonstrate how this can make a difference, let's flood-fill the selected regions.

22 Choose the ◈ **Flood Fill** tool with **Tolerance** set to 100, and pick a bold colour from the **Colour** tab. Click in the square selection region.

The principle at work here is that partially selected pixels are only partially affected by manipulations you apply (like flooding them with paint).

Now that you've seen the principle in action, you're sure to find lots of ways to use partial selections for blends and special effects. It will help when you're working with masks too!

Selection Tools

Well, that completes our survey of the basic selection tools.

- To learn about creating selections from paths, see the "Using Paths" tutorial.
- For information about the  **Magnetic Selection Tool**, the **Extract** command, and creating selections from a mask or alpha channel see the *PhotoPlus User Guide* and online Help.

Adjustable Selection tools

In this tutorial, we've dealt with 'all-or-nothing' selections. Even with the **Colour Selection** tool, any pixel inside the selection bounding box is 100% selected. But selection, like lightness, can have 'shades of grey.'

Having variable levels of selection means that operations carried out in the selected area will vary in strength. It's not always easy to see when pixels aren't fully selected, because the selection bounding box alone won't tell you. But PhotoPlus provides a selection mode that not only reveals partial selections, but lets you create them...

Like the **Text Selection** tool, the **Adjustable Selection** tools are a way to create selections using the same techniques you'd otherwise use to create solids. Likewise, they're useful when you want to fill or carve out something solid without using a separate text or shape layer.

To try them, click the **Adjustable Selection** tools flyout.

For more information, see online Help.

Colour Spaces

In this tutorial, we'll investigate Greyscale, HSL, RGB, and CMYK colour modes.

You will:

- Use the PhotoPlus Colour Mode selector to switch between colour modes.

- Learn about hue, saturation, and lightness.

- Work with the Adjust Colour dialog.

- Learn how your computer stores colour information.

Colour Spaces

In the next few pages, we'll explore the PhotoPlus colour selection dialogs. In particular, we'll see what they can teach us about two different colour spaces: HSL and RGB. If you've never had a colour theory class, take this opportunity to learn what those letters mean. No prerequisites here—just follow along carefully, and you'll gain more confident control over your creative output.

Let's begin with the simplest mode: Greyscale. (Don't be deceived—a century and a half of black-and-white photography produced relatively few masters, so it can't be all that simple!)

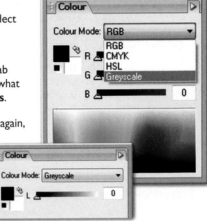

1 Click on the PhotoPlus **Colour** tab and select **Greyscale** from the **Colour Mode** list.

The sample spectrum remains in colour. However, instead of three sliders on the tab there's now only one, labelled **L**, because what the slider manipulates is actually **Lightness**.

2 Drag the slider from left to right and back again, watch the upper foreground colour swatch and the value readout next to the slider.

You'll see that there's no 'colour' as such, only shades of grey. With the slider at the left end, the swatch is black and the readout says 0—no lightness, full black. At the right end of the scale, it's 255—maximum lightness, full white.

3 Move your cursor down to the colour spectrum sample, where it will change to a ✐ dropper icon. Move it up and down within the spectrum, and then from side to side. This time, watch the sample swatch that pops up just above the spectrum. What happens there?

> ⓘ Technically speaking, we should be careful about stating that there's 'no colour' in greyscale mode. As we'll see by the end of this tutorial, these 256 discrete shades of grey are each colours in their own right.

You can see that the up-and-down movement affects the lightness output level just as dragging the slider did. Up means lighter; down means darker.

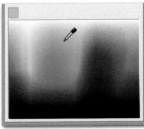

You can think of the spectrum box as a graph, with lightness as the vertical or Y axis. But what about the X axis? In greyscale mode, side-to-side motion doesn't change the output value at all. Still, can you hazard a guess as to what property varies along the horizontal axis?

Colour Spaces

If you answered "colour," you deserve partial credit. Certainly, the spectrum does vary from left to right through the 'colours' of the rainbow. But in fact, it's *all* colour: even grey values can be said to have colour. The more precise term for what most of us loosely call 'colour' is **Hue**. So with **L** for lightness and **H** for hue we now have two-thirds of HSL mode, which is the next stop on our tour.

4 Before leaving greyscale mode, drag the **L** (lightness) slider so it's approximately one-quarter of the way from the left (a value of around 64). Now select **HSL** as the colour mode.

Before making any further adjustments, notice that upper **H** slider (the H stands for hue) has its own mini-rainbow, corresponding to the horizontal axis of the spectrum box.

Also, notice that the **L** slider is positioned about one-quarter of the way along, with a value of 25; the maximum value being 100 in this mode.

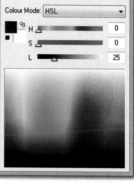

5 Drag the **L** slider to the middle of its range (roughly 50), and switch back to Greyscale mode.

You'll see that the **L** slider there has moved correspondingly.

6 Switch back to **HSL** mode and hover the cursor around the spectrum box while watching the sample swatch.

As you might expect, up-and-down movement still varies the sample's lightness, while left-to-right movement now varies its hue.

7 Drag the **H** slider from side to side.

If you've been following instructions, the foreground colour is still stuck at a middle grey value. Why doesn't it change at this point? Hint: Take a look at that middle **S** slider, which is still all the way to the left, at the 0 value.

8 Drag the **S** slider very slowly to the right while watching the foreground swatch. What's happening?

At the leftmost (0) value, you'll see the swatch is pure grey, with no hue. At the rightmost (100) value, it might be described as pure hue, or as a maximum intensity of the selected hue. In between, it's apparently a mixture of hue and grey.

So what does the S stand for? **Saturation**—so put another way, the slider varies the colour output between 'unsaturated' and 'fully saturated.'

Colour Spaces

9 Try this: While holding down the left mouse button, move the cursor around in the spectrum sample. This actually updates the foreground colour *and* all three sliders in real time. Keep an eye on the value readouts.

Note that the **S** slider jumps right away to 100 and stays there, as long as you're picking up a colour from the spectrum box. That's consistent with the spectrum representing just two of the three dimensions, while the third—saturation—is held constant at 100%.

10 One more experiment in HSL mode. Place the **H** and **S** sliders somewhere in the middle, then drag the **L** slider to maximum. Now the foreground colour becomes pure white, and no amount of **H** or **S** adjustment makes a difference. You'll get a comparable result (i.e., solid black) when **L** is set to minimum, proving how the **L** control (like **S**) exerts a dominant influence at either end of its range.

11 Click the foreground colour sample to open the **Adjust Colour** dialog.

12 Drag the red dot in the centre square down to the lower left corner as far as it will go. Now take a look at the HSL readout values.

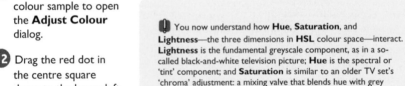

 You now understand how **Hue**, **Saturation**, and **Lightness**—the three dimensions in **HSL** colour space—interact. **Lightness** is the fundamental greyscale component, as in a so-called black-and-white television picture; **Hue** is the spectral or 'tint' component; and **Saturation** is similar to an older TV set's 'chroma' adjustment: a mixing valve that blends hue with grey tones.

Saturation is at 0 (minimum), while lightness is at 255 (maximum).

Remembering what you've recently seen on the **Colour** tab, the values should tell you there's no hue information getting through, in fact nothing but white in the output colour—and sure enough, that's what's showing in the **Current Colour** box.

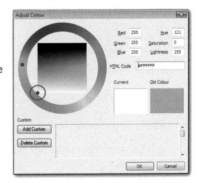

Colour Spaces

The centre square is basically a graph, comparable to the **Colour** tab's spectrum, with lightness plotted vertically and saturation (rather than hue) shown horizontally.

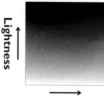

13 Demonstrate all this to yourself by dragging the red dot around the square's edges and interior, while checking the readout. No matter where you move the dot, the hue value won't move!

14 Hue, of course, is represented by the rainbow band that encircles the square—as dragging the other red dot around will quickly prove.

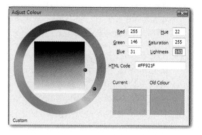

Leaving aside the fact that in nature the wavelengths of visible light don't simply 'wrap around' to meet each other, this is a great way to depict all three components. Great for a human interface at least—but not for a computer, which relies on the **RGB** system to describe the same gamut of colours as **HSL**.

15 Notice the **Red**, **Green**, and **Blue** values to the left of the **HSL** values in the dialog. Before you start experimenting, you might want to read a bit further.

RGB is based on the principle of mixing red, green, and blue—the three primary colours (wavelengths of light, actually)—in varying proportions to achieve other colours. Mix all three equally, and you get white; turn all off and you get black.

But computers only understand **bits**, not colours. **24 bit** colour on a computer uses 8 bits to encode each of the three channels: storing 256 possible levels (0-255) for each channel. An RGB value of "0,0,0" represents pure black; a value of "255,255,255" represents pure white.

> Wondering what the **Adjust Colour** dialog's **HTML Code** box is showing you? Web pages also use RGB values, expressed as hexadecimal (base 16) equivalents. For example, white (255,255,255) is represented as #FFFFFF; black (0,0,0) as #000000.

And so back to the colour wheel: Now that you know your way around the HSL space, you can experiment with various combinations to test the claims we've just made. For example, try to achieve a 'pure' red colour (255,0,0). And note that shades of grey can also be described using equal measures of R, G, and B: just keep the square's red dot all the way left so that saturation is 0.

Colour Spaces

To conclude this tutorial, we'll take a moment to discuss the fourth (and very different) colour mode supported by PhotoPlus—**CMYK**.

16 Back on the **Colour** tab, in the **Colour Mode** drop-down list, select **CMYK**.

Notice that there are now four sliders, labelled **C**, **M**, **Y**, and **K**, displayed.

The CMYK colour model is used for preparing printed work, where ink on paper is the medium that determines colour reproduction.

The four process inks are **Cyan**, **Magenta**, **Yellow**, and **BlacK** (Black is referred to as **Key**). Mix these four inks, and you get black. No ink gives you white (i.e., the colour of the paper)—so if you want white, you must use no ink and let the paper show through! In this subtractive model, the more ink applied, the less light reflected, hence the darker the colour.

> **Printing CMYK colour separations**
>
> PhotoPlus supports CMYK output of process colour separations. You can find more information on this in the online Help "Printing" topic, and in the "Printing Photographs" tutorial (in the **Getting Started** sequence).

In PhotoPlus, the C, M, Y, and K channel values are given as percentages, from 0 to 100%.

As you might expect from our descriptions of CMYK and RGB, when it comes to colour reproduction, printing devices and computer screens are on totally different 'wavelengths.' Printing creates colours by mixing inks which absorb light, while a monitor produces an image by mixing the light itself—as R, G, and B primary colours. The variable brightness of each element gives the typical computer monitor a range of colours much greater than can be printed with CMYK inks.

The fundamental differences between the CMYK and RGB colour models, and the limited gamut of the printed page compared to the computer screen, create a colour matching problem: the challenge of getting your printed output to match what you see in your on-screen design. By calibrating your equipment and using great care, you can achieve a close approximation—but you should always verify and never simply assume that the colours on your screen will turn out exactly the same when printed.

> For more accurate RGB - CMYK colour matching, we recommend that you take advantage of the PhotoPlus colour management features. For details, see "Colour concepts" in online Help.

Use the PhotoPlus Export Optimizer to compare the properties of popular graphic file formats.

In this tutorial, you will:

- Work with the Export Optimizer dialog.

- Explore the differences between BMP, GIF, and JPG file formats.

- Learn about bit depth, colour palettes, and dithering.

- Work with layers and transparency.

Note: The material covered here illustrates concepts explained in more depth in the *PhotoPlus User Guide*, and in the "Colour Concepts" topic of online Help.

Image Formats

In PhotoPlus, the **Save** command always stores an image in the native PhotoPlus SPP format, while the **Export** command lets you output to any of the conventional graphic file formats, such as JPEG, GIF, TIFF, or PNG. This tutorial explores the **Export Optimizer** that is integrated with the export function, and which literally provides a window on different image formats and their settings.

1 Choose **File/Open...** or select **open saved work** from the Startup Wizard. Browse to your **Tutorials/Workspace** folder and open **Gerbera.jpg**. In a standard installation you'll find this folder in the following location.

C:\Program Files\Serif\PhotoPlus\X2\Tutorials\Workspace

BMP format

Windows Bitmap (BMP) files are an historic, but still commonly used, file format for the Windows operating system. Images saved in the .BMP format can range from black and white (1 byte per pixel) up to 24 bit colour (16.7 million colours).

2 Choose **Export Optimizer...** from the **File** menu. Click the ⬜ **Single View** button and, in the **Options** tab on the right, select **BMP** from the **Format** list. Under **Bit Depth**, select **24**; most other options will be unavailable.

You're now looking at the original image as it would appear when converted to the standard BMP format using 24 bits per pixel. Doesn't look any different, does it? That's because with these settings, the image itself is in fact the same.

But can you spot something that is different? (Look in the lower left corner.) You may have noticed that the JPG file we loaded occupied about 167 KB on disk, whereas the same file exported as a BMP file would swell to 563 KB! How can this be?

Each particular image format was invented for a reason. BMP, an old standard for image storage on Windows computers, preserves image quality but can do very little to reduce file size. When switching between image formats, there will always be this trade-off between quality and size. Hence the need to **optimize** images: to achieve the best quality in the least amount of disk space, within whatever constraints (such as number of colours) the task may impose.

> 🛈 The number of bits used to define each pixel in an image—the **Bit Depth**—is given by a number, for example, 24-bit colour, 8-bit colour, 8-bit grayscale, etc. The greater the bit depth (the bigger the number), the greater the number of tones (grayscale or colour) that can be represented. Digital images may be produced in black and white, grayscale, or colour.

Image Formats

3 Continue by selecting a **Bit Depth** value of **8**.

8 bits can only store 256 values, so each pixel in the image is now limited to one of only 256 possible colour states. (Those 256 unique colours are referred to as a **palette**.) Since this particular test image originally used over 100,000 different colours, the **Export Optimizer** has had to discard nearly all of them... it's amazing how little the image appears to have changed! Still, we can see slight speckling in various places. The estimated file size has dropped to 189 KB.

8-Bit Ordered Dither

4 Choose the **Export Optimizer's** 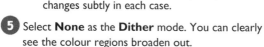 **Zoom** tool and left-click once on the image for a closer view.

Below the **Bit Depth** group, the settings should be **Palette: Optimized** and **Dither: Error Diffusion**.

- Select **Ordered** dithering.

  The image looks subtly different, but not necessarily better or worse.

- Click again on the image to zoom in another notch.

8-Bit Error Diffusion Dither

- Now switch back and forth between the two dither types and note how the pixel pattern changes subtly in each case.

5 Select **None** as the **Dither** mode. You can clearly see the colour regions broaden out.

Right-click a couple of times to restore the 100% zoom view and click between 24-bit and 8-bit and evaluate.

No Dither (None)

Dithering is a way of fooling the eye into perceiving more colours where fewer are actually present. Adjacent lighter and darker pixels, for example, create the impression of shading that may not really be there. **Ordered** dithering imposes a subtle grid-like pattern, but it removes most of the speckling that results from the **Error Diffusion** method. Which technique to use depends greatly on the specific image. As a general rule, whenever you're reducing the number of colours in a full-colour photographic image, it's almost mandatory to apply one of the two dithering schemes or the result won't look right at all. (If the image has fewer colours to start with, that's a different story.)

Image Formats

6 Using **Ordered** dithering, select a **Bit Depth** of **4**. This means only 16 colours are used. Now select 1 as the **Bit Depth**. Only two colours remain: PhotoPlus has chosen pink and purple. Compare the two dither modes now. **Error Diffusion** preserves the subject matter more clearly. Switch back to 8-bit mode.

You might use the **Export Optimizer** itself as a way of applying a special effect (like this two-colour dither) at the last minute.

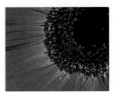

4-Bit Ordered Dither

1-Bit Ordered Dither

GIF format

Next we'll look at the popular .GIF format which, like BMP, is 'lossless'—it doesn't discard any pixel information. Unlike BMP, the GIF format excels at reducing file size using compression algorithms and so is one standard for Web images.

7 In the **Format** list, select **GIF**, and ensure **Ordered** dithering is selected.

1-Bit Error Diffusion Dither

GIF's major drawback is that it's limited to a maximum of 256 colours: when exporting to GIF, the image is never going to look better than it did as an 8-bit BMP, however, the image size is now only 112 KB, about 40% less than before—and we're not done by any means.

GIF with 32 Colour Ordered Dither

A few things to note about the **GIF** format. Firstly, it's ideal for greyscale images, which by definition won't have more than 256 colours to start with. Second, you can check the **Transparent** setting to preserve clear pixels or 'holes' in your image. Finally, you won't lose anything by selecting **Interlaced** if your images are intended for the Web; this means the image will be initially displayed at full size, but at an increasingly better resolution as more and more of the image is downloaded.

8 In the **Colours** list, you can choose any power of 2 up to 256 (a range that corresponds to Bit Depth settings of 1 to 8). Choose **128** and inspect the image, then choose **64**, and then **32**. Now we've reduced the image size to 49 KB and still the image looks passable!

> We mentioned that 256 unique colours comprise a palette. You'll notice that besides the **Optimized** palette setting we've been applying so far (which lets PhotoPlus pick the 256 best colours for rendering the image), a **Web palette** is also available. A Web palette is a standard set of 216 specific colours that you should use only if you know for sure that people viewing your images in a Web browser will be limited to a 256-colour monitor. You can read more about this in the *PhotoPlus User Guide* or online Help.

JPEG format

The .JPG or .JPEG (Joint Photographic Experts Group) file format, like .GIF, is universally supported in Web browsers. Unlike .GIF, it encodes 24-bit images but is a lossy format depending on the selected compression setting. .JPG is clearly the format of choice for full-colour photographic images. For black and white (256-level, 8-bit greyscale) photos, it has no particular advantages over .GIF.

9 In the **Format** list, now select **JPEG**.

Here there's only one major adjustment, a **Quality** slider—no bit depth option this time. JPEG is a 24-bit standard intended for photographs. This format achieves remarkable file size reduction by discarding detail; hence it's known as a 'lossy' compression scheme. Even with a **Quality** setting of 100%, our image is only 100 KB in size.

JPEG Quality: 100%

10 Drag the **Quality** slider all the way down to 0%. The file size is now only 13 KB now but it looks terrible!

Whereas the dithered colour reductions in the other formats had a 'Special Effects' feel, this low-resolution photographic reproduction is simply awful; not something likely to impress viewers on a Web site. It's a reference image at best.

JPEG Quality: 0%

11 Starting with the slider at the low end, gradually drag it higher until you've reached an acceptable quality level.

> Assuming your goal is to compress the image as much as possible while retaining acceptable quality, this threshold-finding approach is a reasonable one when exporting to the JPEG format. Or you can just as well work down from 100% to find an acceptable value.

Image Formats

Transparency

Let's conclude this survey of the **Export Optimizer** by looking at a different kind of dithering—this time as applied to transparency, to achieve smooth-looking edges. First, we'll need to introduce some transparency into our sample image.

12 Click **Cancel** to close the **Export Optimizer**. On the **Layers** tab at the right of the workspace, right-click over the **Background** layer in the Layer Manager, and then select **Promote to Layer**.

This creates a standard layer (which supports transparency) from the original **Background** layer which doesn't. The next step simply adds some transparency by creating a 'feathered' selection that fades off gradually toward the edges.

13 On the ▣▾ Standard Selection Tools flyout, click the ◯ **Ellipse Selection** tool. On the context toolbar, set the **Feather** value to 15 pixels.

Drag out a circular selection in the middle of the image. The circle will expand after you release the mouse button to include the extra 15 pixels of 'feathered' area.

Within that feathered region, pixels are partially selected— more so toward the centre, less so toward the edge. You won't see any fade-off yet because the entire image is still present, but that's about to change!

14 On the **Select** menu, choose **Invert**.

Inverting the selection has flipped each pixel's level of selection, i.e., if a pixel was completely selected, it's now completely deselected; if it was 40% selected, it's now 40% deselected (60% selected), and so on.

15 Press the **Delete** key

What have we taken away? All of the outside pixels that were deselected before we inverted the selection, and progressively less (moving toward the centre) of each partially selected 'feathered' pixel. The technique we've used has partially erased sections of the original image, leaving a nicely graduated transparent edge we can now experiment with.

If transparency is new to you, you can see how a graphic designer might strive to achieve (and would want to preserve) this edge transparency in order to blend the graphic with a background—for example, on a Web page or in another more complex image. On this note, we can head back to the **Export Optimizer**.

16 Open the **Export Optimizer**. With the **GIF** format selected, select the **Transparent** check box to enable transparency for this export. In the adjacent drop-down list, you'll already recognize the dithering choices. Choose **Error Diffusion**.

17 Clear the **Transparent** box for now, and select the **Matte** box.

The **Matte** setting gives the **Export Optimizer** control over the background of the image. You'll notice straight away that the feathered edge information of your image is now incorporated into the colour-backed export. The exported feathering dithers from your original image information to a solid colour specified by the **Matte**, shown by the colour swatch next to the **Matte** checkbox. Selecting a colour here allows your image to blend to an existing known background, such as on a Web page you are designing, without having to alter your original image.

18 Change the **Matte** colour to red by clicking on the white sample in the **Export Optimizer** dialog. Your blended transparent image now magically blends to a red background, all without editing the image!

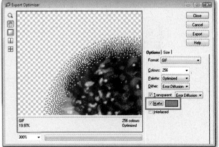

19 Select the **Transparency** box while the **Matte** setting is still selected. You'll notice that the solid transparency of the GIF format still dithers to a faked soft edge, and that the edge is also still red—versatile control for your Web pages! Experiment with other formats, too. Formats that support variable transparency, like TIF and PNG, can produce some truly beautiful results for your printed material and Web pages alike.

> GIFs only support single-level transparency: their pixels must be either wholly transparent or wholly opaque. As such, GIF might not be the export format of choice for our variably transparent sample graphics. But rather than force you to use a different format, the **Export Optimizer** can dither the transparency channel so as to 'fake' a blended transparency. This at least gives you the option of using GIF for its other advantages (losslessness, browser support, etc.).

Image Formats

We hope we've convinced you of how useful the **Export Optimizer** can be. We've used it only in ▦ **Single View** mode, but you can also select ▥ **Double** or ▦ **Quad View** (illustrated right) to compare image quality using two or four different settings and/or formats.

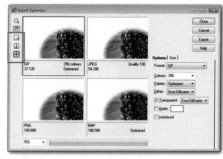

Once you've found a preferred combination, select it and click the **Export** button to proceed to file saving.

To apply the same export settings next time, you don't need to use the **Export Optimizer** again; simply choose **File/Export**.

The formats explored here are just some of those available in PhotoPlus. We support over 20 image export formats including lossless export options for JPEG2000 (JP2 and J2K), Adobe® Photoshop®, and formats for animations!

Brush Tips and Tricks

Explore the range and scope of the Brush Options that can be set for many of the tools used in PhotoPlus.

In this tutorial, you will:

- Work with the Paintbrush tool.
- Explore the Brush Tip tab.
- Experiment with Brush Options dialog settings.
- Create a custom brush tip.

Brush Tips and Tricks

Brush is a property of a large number of the tools used in PhotoPlus (Background Eraser, Blur, Burn, Clone, Dodge, Paintbrush, Pattern, Scratch Remover, Sharpen, Smudge, Sponge, Standard Eraser, Warp). By exploring some of the basic Brush Options using the basic Paintbrush, you can give yourself a solid foundation for mastering many of the PhotoPlus tools and hopefully have a bit of fun along the way.

1 In the Startup Wizard, click **create new picture** (or from the **File** menu, click **New**, then **create new picture**). In the **New Image** dialog, create a new picture with plenty of space (say 600 x 600 pixels) and a white background.

2 On the **File** menu, click **Preferences**.

In the **Preferences** dialog, on the **General** tab, ensure that **Brush Size** is selected and click **OK**. This gives you a circular cursor that reflects the current brush size.

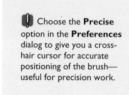 Choose the **Precise** option in the **Preferences** dialog to give you a cross-hair cursor for accurate positioning of the brush—useful for precision work.

3 On the Tools toolbar, select the ✏ **Paintbrush** tool.

On the **Brush Tip** tab, select **Basic** from the drop-down list of categories. In the samples gallery, scroll down past the soft brushes to the set of hard brushes, and click on the 64-pixel brush.

At the top of the workspace, the Brush context toolbar updates to show the selected brush properties.

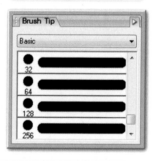

4 To customize the current brush, click its sample on the Brush context toolbar to open the **Brush Options** dialog.

In the **Attributes** list, click each item in turn and apply the following settings:

- **Size:** Diameter 64
- **Spacing:** Spacing 20, Dab Count 1
- **Shape:** Hardness 100, Angle 0, Roundness 100

You'll see that some other properties are presently set to **None**, indicating no effect.

The **Colour** and **Texture** attributes are currently unselected and therefore have no effect either.

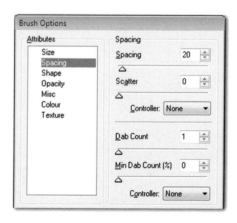

Brush Tips and Tricks

Also note that some of the brush settings include a **Controller** option. This allows you to control the brush stroke using variations in the direction of the brush, a pressure-sensitive tablet, or even a random value. We'll explore this later.

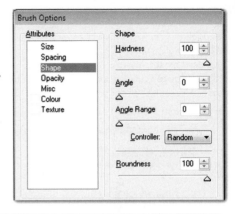

5 Close the **Brush Options** dialog when you've finished exploring.

6 On the **Colour** tab, click the foreground swatch.

Changes you make to the current brush via the Brush context toolbar only affect the *current brush*. Brushes in the **Brush Tip** tab galleries are stored separately.

After customizing a brush, you can save it as a gallery brush in a **user-created category**:

1. To add a new user-created category, click the **Brush Tip Tab Menu** arrow button (in the upper right corner of the tab), and select **Add Category**.

2. When you've created your category, it displays automatically in the category drop-down list. Right-click in the gallery and select **New Brush**.

3. Name your brush and then click **OK**. Your new brush is added to your new user-created category.

In the **Adjust Colour** dialog, click in the colour wheel to select a foreground colour for your brush, then click **OK**.

Position your cursor over the page, then click and release. This is like touching the tip of a paintbrush to a sheet of paper.

Now click and drag to paint a brush stroke across the page.

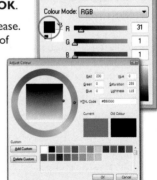

The continuous appearance of the stroke is an illusion.

PhotoPlus brush strokes are a sequence of discrete brush tip marks—if the marks are close enough together, the stroke looks solid. In the **Brush Options** dialog, you can change the spacing between brush tip marks to give the appearance of a continuous stroke or a dotted line.

Brush Tips and Tricks

7 On the Brush context toolbar, click the Brush sample to open the **Brush Options** dialog.

In the **Attributes** list:

- Select **Spacing** and drag the **Spacing** slider gradually to the right while observing the effect in the preview window: you'll see the marks spreading out.
- Set the slider to **100** (the setting is a percentage of brush diameter) and click **OK**.

Now paint another line across the image.

From here we can explore the effect of the other **Spacing** attributes on the **Brush Options** dialog.

8 In the **Brush Options** dialog:

- Select the **Size** attribute. Set **Diameter** to **32**.
- Select the **Spacing** attribute. Set **Scatter** to **200**; set **Scatter Controller** to **Random**.

Once you've added a control input to vary the scatter property, you'll see the brush marks diverge from their formerly straight path.

Click **OK** and paint another line across the page.

9 Open the **Brush Options** dialog again and select the **Spacing** attribute. So far we've left the **Dab Count** set at **1**. In PhotoPlus a single mark can consist of as few as one, or as many as 20 dabs. Raising the dab count produces a more ragged stroke.

- Leave the **Scatter** setting of **200** but increased the **Dab Count** setting to **5**.

Click **OK** and paint another line across the page.

> Note that raising the dab count without scattering the dabs, or otherwise varying the stroke, usually has a negligible effect.

If you leave the **Dab Count Controller** at **None**, you'll get the specified number of dabs with each mark. Choosing **Random** varies the number of dabs per mark randomly—between the **Dab Count** and **Min Dab Count** settings.

Now let's explore more of the **Shape** attributes of the **Brush Options**...

10 In the **Brush Options** dialog:

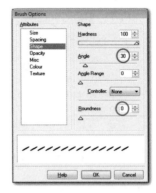

- Select the **Spacing** attribute and set the **Scatter Controller** to **None**, with **Spacing** at **100**.

- Select the **Shape** attribute and drag the **Roundness** slider to the left while observing the effect in the preview window. The lower you go, the less height the brush has, relative to width.

  Slide the setting down to **0**, then drag the **Angle** slider to 'spin' the brush.

  Set **Angle** to **30**.

  Click **OK** and paint another line across the page.

11 Drag the **Spacing** slider back to **1** and you now have a basic calligraphic pen. Try writing your name with it.

Set the **Spacing** back to **100** , and the **Dab Count** to **1**.

12 Select the **Shape** attribute:

- Set the **Angle Range Controller** to **Random**.

- Move the **Angle Range** slider up and down while watching the preview window. Set the slider to **180**.

- Click **OK** and paint a line across the page.

> You'll find a selection of preset calligraphic pen samples on the **Brush Tip** tab, in the **Calligraphic** category.

As you can see we have introduced random rotational variation within the specified range—a sort of rotational scatter. (This is most effective when used in conjunction with actual Scatter.)

Next, we'll look at the **Hardness** property of the **Shape** attribute.

So far in this tutorial we have been using a **Hardness** setting of **100**, which produces a sharp-edged line like that of a pen or pencil. By reducing the **Hardness** value we can define a progressively softer-edged brush, that is, one with a solid centre and feathered (semi-transparent) edge.

Brush Tips and Tricks

13 Return to the **Brush Tip** tab and display the **Basic** gallery. Click on the soft 64-pixel brush.

In the **Brush Options** dialog, in the **Shape** attributes, you'll see that this brush tip has a **Hardness** setting of **5**.

Paint another line across the page.

Soft-edged brushes like this are indispensable (especially with reduced **Opacity** settings) for making subtle painting changes, erasing around edges, and so on.

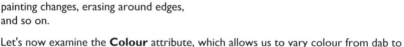

Let's now examine the **Colour** attribute, which allows us to vary colour from dab to dab.

14 On the **Brush Tip t**ab, in the **Calligraphic** category, select the 50-pixel sample.

In the **Brush Options** dialog:

- Select the **Spacing** attribute and set the **Spacing** to **5**,
- Select the **Shape** attribute and set the **Angle** to **90**, the **Roundness** to **0**, and **Hardness** to **100**.
- Select the check box next to the **Colour** attribute and then set all three **Deviation** sliders to **100** to see the effect.

Now vary each of the three **Deviation** settings independently while watching the preview at the bottom of the dialog. (Your actual effects will differ depending on the current colour selected.)

Paint three lines across the page, one with each slider set to **100** while the other two are set to **0**.

100% Hue Deviation

100% Saturation Deviation

100% Brightness Deviation

Brush Tips and Tricks

Opacity is one of the basic properties you can set for the current brush using the Brush context toolbar. The **Brush Options** dialog also provides an **Opacity Controller** that uses an input to vary the opacity from one brush dab to another.

15 In the **Brush Options** dialog, clear the **Colour** attribute and then select **Opacity**.

In the **Controller** box, select **Random**.

Click **OK** and paint a line across the page.

The opacity for each dab is varied randomly between **0** and the value set in the Brush context toolbar.

16 Back in the **Brush Options** dialog:

- Select **Opacity** and select **Fade** in the **Controller** box.
- Select a **Fade** value of **40** steps.
- Click **OK** and paint a line across the page.

Now the brush stroke fades linearly from the **Opacity** value set on the Brush context toolbar down to **0** in the number of steps specified (in this case, 40).

Finally, lets look at the effect of the **Texture** attribute.

17 On the **Brush Tip** tab, select the soft 64-pixel brush from the **Basic** category. In the **Brush Options** dialog, select the **Texture** check box and then click the square pattern sample (which may be blank to start with) to open the **Patterns** dialog.

Select any pattern (right-click to change categories) and click **OK**.

Click **OK** to close the dialog and paint a line across the page. The selected pattern is included in your painting!

If the large range of basic brush tips provided on the **Brush Tip** tab isn't sufficient, it is a simple job to create your own brushes. You can create a brush from any selected design—let's try one using the heart shape as an example.

Brush Tips and Tricks

To create a custom brush

1 On the **Colour** tab, select your foreground colour.

(We've used red, but you should note that the colour you choose will directly impact the maximum opacity of the resulting brush. For a full opaque brush, set the foreground colour to 100% black.)

2 On the Tools toolbar, on the QuickShapes flyout, select the **Heart**.

When adding a QuickShape, we can choose to add it as a new **Shape Layer**, a new **Path**, or simply add it to the current layer (as a **Fill Bitmap**); these options are displayed on the context toolbar.

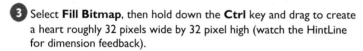

3 Select **Fill Bitmap**, then hold down the **Ctrl** key and drag to create a heart roughly 32 pixels wide by 32 pixel high (watch the HintLine for dimension feedback).

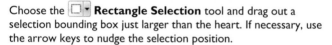

Choose the ⬚▾ **Rectangle Selection** tool and drag out a selection bounding box just larger than the heart. If necessary, use the arrow keys to nudge the selection position.

4 On the **Brush Tip** tab, right-click and select **Add Category**.

In the **New Category** dialog, name the new brush category and click **OK**.

In the **Brush Tip** tab category drop-down list, select your new category.

5 Right-click in the Brush Tip gallery and choose **Define Brush**.

In the **New Brush** dialog, type a name for your new brush and click **OK**.

Your new brush appears in the **Brush Tip** tab gallery, in your user-created category. (Hover over the sample to reveal the brush name.)

6 Press **Ctrl+D** to remove any selection still present. Select the **Paintbrush** tool and select your new brush tip.

On the **Brush Tip** tab, right-click your new brush and select **Brush Options**.

Set the attributes to your liking (try increasing the **Spacing** and **Dab Count**.)

7 You can now use your new brush to paint on your page.

It is impossible to cover the full range and scope of the PhotoPlus **Brush Options** dialog. Having worked through these exercises, however, you're now well equipped to build on the fundamentals and continue exploring other brush tip permutations and combinations.

Photography

In this section, you'll find a collection of tutorials aimed at helping you get the most out of your digital images.

- **Colouring Black and White Images**
- **Recolouring Images**
- **Replacing Photo Backgrounds**
- **Retouching Photographs**
- **Repairing and Restoring Photographs**
- **Making Contrast Adjustments**
- **Creating Macros and Batch Processing**

Colouring Black and White Images

Turn a photo into a modern, stylish digital creation by adding a splash of colour to greyscale images. This relatively simple tutorial shows the ease with which colour can be added to a greyscale image.

In this tutorial, you'll learn how to:

- Convert a colour image to greyscale.

- Add layers and change layer properties.

- Work with blend modes.

- Adjust settings on the Brush Tip and Colour tabs.

- Use the Paintbrush tool to apply colour to a layer.

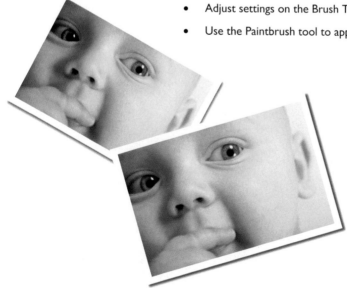

Colouring Black and White Images

Add a splash of colour to greyscale images—turn a photo into a modern, stylish digital creation. This relatively simple tutorial shows the ease with which colour can be added to a greyscale image.

1 Click **File**, then **Open**, browse to the **Tutorials/Workspace** folder and open the **Baby.jpg** file.

In a standard installation, you'll find this in the following location:

C:\Program Files\Serif\PhotoPlus\X2\Tutorials\Workspace

If you're using one of your own images, you can make a greyscale version by clicking **Image**, then **Adjust**, then **Greyscale**. The image will still have RGB components so you can add colour to it.

2 On the **Layers** tab, click the ⊞ **New Layer** button to add a new layer.

In the **Layer Properties** dialog:

- Name your layer 'Add colour.'
- Set the **Blend Mode** to **Colour**.
- Leave the **Opacity** at 100%.

3 Select the ✎ **Paintbrush** tool.

On the **Brush Tip** tab, in the **Basic** brush types list, you'll find soft and hard brushes, listed in that order, in sizes from 1 to 256 pixels. Choose an appropriate size soft brush tip for the area you want to colour. We chose a 16 pixel brush.

A layer's **blend mode** determines how each pixel on that layer visibly combines with those on layers below. (Because there are no layers below the **Background** layer, it can't have a blend mode.) Changing a layer's blend mode property doesn't alter the pixels on the layer—so you can create different blend mode effects, then merge layers when you've achieved the result you want.

When you select the **Colour** blend mode, the result is a combination of the hue and saturation of the top colour with the lightness of the bottom colour. Because lightness values (greyscale levels) are preserved, this mode is useful for tinting greyscale images.

For more information see "Using blend modes" in online Help.

Colouring Black and White Images

4 Use the 🔍 **Zoom** tool to zoom into the area around one of the eyes.

5 On the **Colour** tab, in the **Colour Mode** drop-down list, select **RGB**.

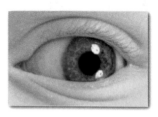

Set the foreground colour to **R=0, G=86, B=246**, and start painting around the eye.

Don't worry about being too accurate with the paintbrush at this stage—the great advantage of painting on a layer is that you can delete any parts that go outside the desired area.

6 Repeat this procedure for the other eye.

The final result should resemble our illustration.

Optional step: As we've applied our colour on a separate layer, we can change the **opacity** of the layer to reduce the intensity of the colour.

To do this:

- On the **Layers** tab, right-click the **Add Colour** layer and select **Properties**.

- In the **Layer Properties** dialog, reduce the **Opacity** value as required (try 75%) and than click **OK**.

When you've finished, why not turn your image into a unique greeting card.

> 💡 You can paint directly on the original image with the **Paintbrush** tool (first promote it to a layer by right-clicking on the **Background** layer on the **Layers** tab and selecting **Promote to Layer**), but this approach is inflexible—you can't change it afterwards. It's much better practice to add a new layer and paint on this new layer. In this way you can add or delete areas without affecting the original image.

Congratulations

Recolouring Images

Ever wanted to spray your car a different colour without the risk and expense? Try it first with a photograph!

In this tutorial, you'll learn how to:

- Recolour an image by adjusting the hue.

- Use the Colour Pickup tool to choose a new foreground colour from the colours available in an image.

- Use the Paintbrush tool to apply colour to areas of an image.

- Adjust settings on the Brush Tip tab and Context toolbar.

Recolouring Images

PhotoPlus provides several different ways to selectively replace colour in an image. In this tutorial, we'll demonstrate one of the easiest methods—adjusting the hue using the **Hue/Saturation/Lightness** dialog.

1 On the Standard toolbar, click  **Open**, or click **File**, then **Open**.

Browse to locate your own image, or browse to the **Tutorials\Workspace** folder and open the **Porsche.jpg** file.

In a default installation, you'll find this folder in the following location:

C:\Program Files\Serif\PhotoPlus\X2\Tutorials\Workspace

2 On the Layers tab, click 🖳 **New Adjustment Layer**. In the adjustments list, choose **Hue/Saturation/Lightness**.

3 In the **Hue/Saturation/Lightness** dialog, in the **Edit** drop-down list, select **Blues** to adjust the range of blue tones in the image (if you leave the setting at **Master**, you will adjust the entire range).

4 In the **Range** spectrum, you'll see a set of 'range indicator' sliders in the blue region, between the two spectrum bars.

These slider pairs show the affected colour ranges at each setting. You can drag these sliders left or right to adjust the extent of each range.

Drag the rightmost pair of sliders further to the right—towards magenta—and drag the leftmost pair further to the left—towards cyan—as in our illustration.

This expands the new colour range to include more shades of blue, creating a more 'feathered' effect rather than a hard-edged tone.

💡 For information about other ways to replace colour in an image, see the following online Help topics:

For the **Replace Colour tool**, see "Retouching."

For the **Replace Colour adjustment** feature, see "Replace Colour and Colour Balance Adjustments."

5 Using the **Hue** slider, adjust the value to **-100** (you can also type directly into the value box). The deep blue paintwork changes to mid-green.

Click **OK** when you are happy with the new colour.

You now have an image of a green Porsche. There are a few minor areas of grey, which haven't been adjusted (since they are not blue). If you'd like these areas to match the green of the bodywork, complete the following optional steps.

6 On the Tools toolbar, click the ![pickup] **Colour Pickup** tool and then click over an area of mid-green on the bodywork to make it the foreground colour.

(To verify this, check the foreground swatch on the **Colour** tab.)

7 Click the ![brush] **Paintbrush** tool.

8 On the **Brush Tip** tab, choose a soft brush tip of size **64** pixels.

9 On the Brush context toolbar, select **Colour** as the blend mode and set the **Opacity** to **100%**.

Paint over grey areas of the bodywork to colour them.

The final result should look similar to our illustration.

Blend Modes

The **Clone** tool's blend mode determines what happens when you use the tool to apply a new colour pixel on top of an existing colour pixel.

In this example, we selected the **Colour** blend mode, which results in a combination of the hue and saturation of the top colour with the lightness of the bottom colour.

For more information, see "Using blend modes" in online Help.

Replacing Photograph Backgrounds

Extract an element from one photo and place it against different backdrops to produce a series of 'faked' photos!

In this tutorial, you'll learn how to:

- Use the Edge Marker tool to outline a subject.

- Adjust settings in the Extraction window.

- Paste an extracted subject into a new image as a new layer.

Replacing Photograph Backgrounds

Work with the Extraction tool and layers to create a series of faked photographs.

1 On the Standard toolbar, click 📄 **Open**. Browse to the **Tutorials/Workspace** folder and open the **Stairs1.jpg** file. In a standard installation, you'll find this file in the following location:

C:\Program Files\Serif\PhotoPlus\X2\Tutorials\Workspace

2 On the **Edit** menu, select **Extract** to open the **Extraction** window.

- To the left of the Preview pane, click the 🔍 **Zoom** tool then click on your image to zoom into it.

- Also on the left, click the ✏️ **Edge Marker** and use it to outline the boy on the left.

- To the right of the Preview pane, set the **Brush Size** to **2**.

Make sure you include the part of the body (foreground) and part of the stairs (background) under the Edge Marker outline, and also draw around any 'gaps' in the subject.

> 💡 To apply instantaneous edge detection as you mark the edge, so that the brush stroke attempts to follow visible edges, select the **Magnetic Edges** box, or **Ctrl**-drag with the **Edge Marker** tool.

You can delete parts of the outline using the ✏️ **Eraser** tool if necessary.

3 Select the ◆ **Foreground** tool, and then click inside the green outline: the inside of the outline turns red to indicate the area to be extracted.

The unmarked region (background) is the area of the photo that will 'disappear.'

4 To the right of the Preview pane, click the **More** button to reveal the advanced extraction settings.

Retouching Photographs

Return to the original **Stairs2.jpg** image. This time, instead of just removing the graze on the boy's chin, we're going to remove him altogether and leave his friend sitting alone on the stairs. We can't do this with the Scratch Remover—it's far too big a job!—so we'll use the  **Clone** tool.

5 The first step is to add a new layer. On the **Layers** tab, click **New Layer** 🔲. In the **Layer Properties** dialog, name the layer '**Cloned Area**.'

We'll now use an area of 'clean' stairs on the left of the photo to clone over the boy and take him out of the picture.

6 On the **Background** layer, select the 🖌 **Clone** tool. This time use a much larger brush tip—around 50 pixels. (You can set this on the Context toolbar.)

- On the context bar, select the **Use all layers** check box.

- Make sure the **Aligned** checkbox is still selected so that each new stroke lines up with the previous one.

- **Shift**-click on the stairs area to define the clone source.

> 💡 It's good practice to make any changes on a new layer so that you can edit your changes without corrupting your original image. You can also subtly change the properties of the layer (Opacity, Blend Mode, Scale, Rotation, etc.) to fine tune your alterations. See "Basics of using layers" in online Help.

7 On the **Cloned Area** layer, make your first clone stroke. This stroke is critical: try and line it up (vertically) with where you 'picked up' your clone source so that the stairs match up. This may take a little practise.

As the area we're trying to cover up is bigger than the area we're sampling you'll have to reset the position of the **Clone** tool a few times.

To do this, clear the **Aligned** box, then click on the layer where you want to start painting, re-select the check box to reset the start position of the brush and carry on painting. In this way, you don't need to define the clone source again. Repeat this process until you have painted over the boy.

If you wish, you can blend the edges of the cloned area with the background by fading out the edge of the area using the 🧽 **Standard Eraser** tool.

You will probably notice that the cloned area is slightly darker than the area of stairs where the boy was sitting—we can easily fix this using an **adjustment filter**.

Retouching Photographs

8 On the **Layers** tab, hide the **Background** layer by clicking the 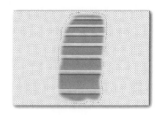 **Hide/Show Layer** button. You will now see just the cloned area.

9 Click the **Cloned Area** layer to make it the active layer, then click the ✎ **Colour Selection** tool. Click on the transparent area surrounding the painted area.

10 On the **Select** menu, choose **Invert**. You've now selected just the cloned area to apply an **adjustment filter** to. (If you don't do this, the adjustment filter will be applied to all the layers and you will not be able to match the two areas.)

11 On the **Layers** tab, display the **Background** layer again by clicking the ◌ button.

12 On the **Image** menu, choose **Adjust** and then select **Brightness/Contrast**. Adjust the sliders until the colour of the selection matches the surrounding area. Click **OK** when you're happy with your changes.

13 Save your file (to a different filename if you wish).

14 Now we'll frame the image using a pre-designed macro.

- Make sure the **Background** layer (original image) is selected on the **Layers** tab.
- Click the **Macros** tab and choose **Frames** from the drop-down list.
- Choose **Metal Frame and Surround** and press the ▷ **Play** button at the bottom of the tab.

  This runs the macro and adds a metal frame and light grey matte to your image.

  Your final image should resemble ours.

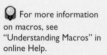 For more information on macros, see "Understanding Macros" in online Help.

For more hands-on experience, see the "Macros and Batch Processing" tutorial.

Repairing and Restoring Photos

We're sure that you have one or two photos or scanned images that are less than perfect. In this tutorial, we'll show you some tips and tricks that we think you'll find useful.

In this exercise, you will:

- Use the Clone tool to remove blemishes from a photo.

- Use a Paint to Select mask and a Curves adjustment to adjust lightness distribution.

- Apply an Unsharp Mask to correct sharpness deficiencies.

Repairing and Restoring Photos

In this two-part tutorial, we'll show you how to repair and restore those less-than-perfect images. In the first section, we'll 'repair' a scanned photo that originally spread across two pages, leaving it with a telltale shadow down the middle. In the second section, we'll correct contrast and sharpness deficiencies—a problem often found in old photographs.

1: Removing blemishes from an image

In this exercise, our goal is to remove the 'gutter mark' running through the centre of the image.

1 On the **File** menu, click **Open**, or select **open saved work** from the Startup Wizard.

Browse to the **Tutorials\Workspace** folder and open **Restore1.jpg**.

The upper section of sky is the easiest part of the image to fix, so we'll start there.

2 On the **Navigator** tab, drag the slider to the right to zoom in to 300%.

3 On the Tools toolbar, click the **✏ Clone** tool, then on the **Brush Tip** tab, select a soft-edged brush.

4 On the Context toolbar:

- Set the brush **Size** to **25** pixels. (In general, the choice of brush size and edge depends on the region you're cloning.)

- Clear the **Aligned** check box.

5 To set the cloning pickup point, press and hold down the **Shift** key and then click just below the top edge of the image, left of the centre shadow line.

Begin the putdown stroke exactly on the shadow. Hold the mouse button down and brush left and right, working down the shadow. Notice that the pickup point moves with you, so you can see where the 'source' of colour is at all times.

Release the button to end the stroke just above the corner of the roof.

> ⓘ The **Aligned** option affects what happens if you use more than one brush stroke:
>
> - In **Aligned mode**, subsequent brush strokes extend the cloned region rather than producing multiple copies.
>
> - In **Non-Aligned mode**, you begin cloning the same pixels all over again from the original pickup point.
>
> For details, see "Cloning a region" in online Help.

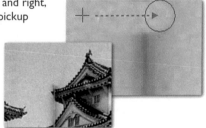

6 Switch to a smaller brush (still soft-edged and non-aligned), and work on the region below the roof corner.

Use short, repeated left-to-right putdown strokes and move from the 'safe' sky in towards the building.

If you make a mistake, you can click **Edit** then **Undo** (**Ctrl+Z**), and **Edit** then **Redo** (**Ctrl+Y**). Toggling between the two is a great way to check your brushwork.

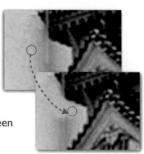

7 For the remainder of the work, set the tool to the **Aligned** mode.

> 🔋 We can get away with using a non-aligned brush repeatedly in this region because there's virtually no detail in the sky. In regions with detail or texture, however, dabbing more than once with a non-aligned tool can destroy the fine-grained, repeating patterns that we perceive as texture, and the result may appear smudged. Because the human eye can be so unforgiving in spotting 'what's wrong with this picture,' it's also important to preserve higher-order structure. For example, if you're cloning foliage, try to maintain natural branching patterns and resist the urge to simply distribute great globs of green.

Using an aligned clone, you can replace a 'damaged' feature with an intact one, and take as many strokes as you need to do it.

The trick is to choose your pickup and putdown points precisely so the cloned feature will blend right in with its surroundings. Don't overextend the strokes trying to get the job done quickly: you may get better results by redefining the pickup point a few times, to 'construct' a new region as a composite of several source regions.

8 Using a very small brush, click for a pickup point at the tip of one of the projecting gable roof tiles.

Choose the putdown point very carefully, envisioning exactly where the cloned projection should go.

Once you're happy with the relative positioning, use a couple of additional strokes to clean up the region below the roof line.

9 Use a similar approach to restore the horizontal roof-edge, and the roof support.

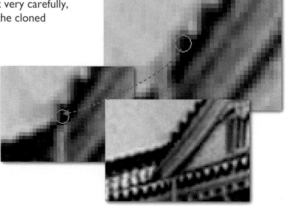

Repairing and Restoring Photos

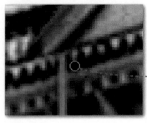

10 Now turn the half-
window into a whole
one, and then finish off
by cloning the
lowermost support (not
shown).

The upper corner of the roof remains a problem area.

You might be tempted to sharpen it up at this point, but before you do, let's take a
closer look at the photograph...

This section is actually missing a projecting element
found on the other roof corners, apparently chopped
off between the pages. No way around it... the image
won't look quite right unless that element is restored.
Is there a similar structure anywhere else in the picture
that might be cloned here? The closest match is a
projection from an opposite tower... but it's pointing
the wrong way. In this case, it's time to abandon the
Clone tool.

11 On the Tools toolbar, click the standard ▢
Rectangle Selection tool, then click and drag to
select the intact roof corner.

Click **Edit**, then click **Copy**.

Click **Edit** again, choose **Paste**, then click **As New Layer**.

The new layer is added to the **Layers** tab and is selected by default.

Repairing and Restoring Photos

12 Press **Ctrl + D** to clear your selection.

13 Working on the new layer, on the **Image** menu, select **Flip Horizontally**, then click **Layer**.

14 On the Tools toolbar, select the ⊕ **Move Tool** to position the selection over the damaged corner. It should fit quite nicely.

15 Once the two layers are well aligned, merge them—right-click the **Layers** tab and select **Merge All**.

16 Finally, use the **Clone** tool again (with a tiny brush) to blend the joined sections.

Your finished image should look similar to ours—a considerable improvement!

We've completed our first exercise in photo restoration—removing blemishes, now let's move on to our second example and a very different challenge.

Repairing and Restoring Photos

2: Correcting contrast and sharpness

In this exercise, we'll turn our attention to a different but equally common problem: how to correct for contrast and sharpness deficiencies. We'll emphasize the **Paint to Select** feature, but you'll also learn some basic techniques you can apply independently.

1 On **the File** menu, click **Open**, or select **open saved work** from the Startup Wizard.

Browse to the **Tutorials\Workspace** folder and open **Restore2.png**.

This old family photo only survived as a colour negative and was recently re-photographed with a digital camera. As you can see, the backlight illumination (using a homemade carrier/backlighting apparatus) was unevenly distributed. Also, the carrier was the wrong size, and there was no colour temperature control.

None of this matters! We'll use PhotoPlus to crop the image, convert it to greyscale, and correct for the uneven lighting.

2 On the Tools toolbar, select the 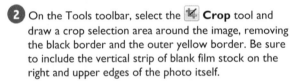 **Crop** tool and draw a crop selection area around the image, removing the black border and the outer yellow border. Be sure to include the vertical strip of blank film stock on the right and upper edges of the photo itself.

Double-click to complete the cropping action. We'll do a more precise crop later.

3 On the **Image** menu, choose **Adjust**, and then select **Negative Image**.

Click **Image**, then **Adjust**, this time selecting **Greyscale**. Click OK to accept the default settings in the Filter Gallery.

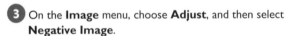

4 Maximize the window containing the image so you have a better view.

Now we have an image, rather than a negative, but obviously not a satisfactory finished image.

The strip down the right (which used to be clear) reveals the most serious problem: an uneven distribution of lightness values resulting from the uneven backlighting. With correct backlighting, this strip should have been all the same grey level.

Repairing and Restoring Photos

As things stand, the upper section of the image is too dark, and the lower section is too light. Whatever contrast or brightness adjustments we apply, we'll need to correct this imbalance first.

We want to boost the lightness at the top, and reduce it at the bottom. The trick is to create a selection that varies between the top and bottom of the image. For example, if the top of the image is relatively more selected than the bottom, and we boost lightness, the top will be lightened more than the bottom.

Using the PhotoPlus **Paint to Select** mode, we can easily create such a selection using a linear gradient.

In the next step, we'll measure the extent of the problem—the process is similar to taking readings with a light meter.

5 On the **Colour** tab, in the **Colour Mode** box, select **Greyscale**. Hover the cursor around the top right corner of the image (in the 'clear' strip) and check the HintLine readout for Grey (which corresponds to lightness). It should read about 50. Take another reading at the bottom of the strip: here, it's about 125.

This spread of values from 50 to 125 represents about 30% of the total possible greyscale range from 0 to 255. That means the approximate correction needed is about 15% lighter at the top and 15% darker at the bottom. Knowing this, we can go ahead and create the gradient selection.

6 On the **Select** menu, check **Paint to Select**.

On the Tools toolbar, on the Fill tools flyout, choose the  **Gradient Fill** tool.

On the Context toolbar, select **Linear** as the fill type, then click the fill sample to display the **Gradient** dialog.

In **Paint to Select** mode, painting with 100% white paint results in a 100% selection, and so on down the grey scale.

The default linear gradient you see in the dialog varies from pure black to pure white, as denoted by the two key colour stops at the lower left and lower right of the gradient.

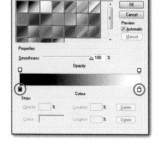

In other words, the black end of the gradient will translate to unselected pixels, while the white end will result in fully selected pixels. The level of selection will vary continuously in between. For more information, see "Modifying a Selection" in online Help.

Repairing and Restoring Photos

In other photo-correction situations, you might want to redefine the gradient: for example, using a 30% grey top end, or a radial fill instead of a linear fill. For our purposes however, the default fill will do fine.

7 Click **Cancel** to close the dialog without any changes.

We'll apply the correction in two passes: once from the top, once from the bottom.

8 Click just below the image and drag to just above it to lay down the black-to-white ("0-to-100") gradient. You'll see the top portion of the image redden, denoting level of selection.

💡 We're assuming here that you're using the default options for Paint to Select mode, and that **Reverse** is not selected on the Context toolbar.

If your image doesn't look like ours, click **Select**, then **Paint to Select Options**, and make sure the **Selected Areas** option is selected.

For more information, see "Modifying a Selection" in online Help.

9 On the **Select** menu, clear the **Paint to Select** option. The result is a selection bounding box around the entire image. What you can't see (but you now know) is that within this area, the level of selection varies from none to all.

10 On the **Image** menu, choose **Adjust**, and then select **Brightness/Contrast**. In the dialog, increase the Brightness value to 15 and click **OK**.

11 Return to **Paint to Select** mode and again select the **Gradient Fill** tool, this time dragging from top to bottom so that the lower portion of the image becomes more selected.

12 Repeat step 10, reducing the **Brightness** value to **-15**. Clear the **Paint to Select** mode, then press **Ctrl+D** to deselect everything.

💡 The advantage of using two half-corrections in opposite directions is that you preserve overall density, avoiding the risk of losing shadow or highlight detail. If you check the lightness levels again, you'll find the top and bottom now measure about 85. The middle of the strip is different because of uneven backlight falloff. You can go back and edit the gradient to achieve more uniform correction if you wish.

Repairing and Restoring Photos

13 Use the **Crop** tool to select only the image area, then double-click to complete the action. Subsequent adjustments will use only the lightness values present in the actual image, not the border.

In this image, your eye tells you that there's no true black or white; hence the image is muddy and low-contrast. Let's see exactly how the lightness values are distributed.

14 Click the **Histogram** tab. In the upper right corner, click the tab menu options button, and select **Show Statistics**.

> The general goal, as in making a photographic print in the darkroom, is to produce a true white, a true black, and a gradation of in-between greys that preserves detail in shadows, highlights, and midtones. Again, in the perfectionist's realm, things are more complicated: you'll need to deal with monitor gamma, printer driver options, paper type... not to mention colour, which is quite another matter! But the fundamentals will always hold true.

You may find it easier to use the histogram if you drag the tab out of its docked state and resize it.

(Your histogram may not look exactly the same as ours, and will vary depending on the cropping initially carried out on the image.)

The plot shows the number of pixels at each possible lightness level from 0 to 255. As you can see, there are no pixels at either the low or high end.

15 Display the **Histogram Tab Menu** and select **Show Statistics**. Move your mouse cursor around the histogram. Notice that the **Count** and **Level** values change.

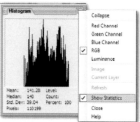

The **Count** value refers to the number of pixels at that current brightness **Level**. At the darkest end of our histogram (a **Level** value of around **60**), there are roughly 0 pixels; at the lightest end (a **Level** value of around **215**) fewer than 15 pixels. Nothing before 63, or after 216. (Your count will vary slightly from these values).

The good news is that the overall distribution of values (represented by the peaks) is fairly even across the range. Sometimes an image will have too many shadow pixels, or too many highlights, and that will often need correcting. In this case, however, we should be able to spread the values out without having to 'tweak' portions of the range.

16 The **Curves** adjustment is an excellent tool to correct lightness distribution. On the **Image** menu, click **Adjust**, and then click **Curves**.

Repairing and Restoring Photos

In the **Curves** dialog, you'll see a diagonal line.

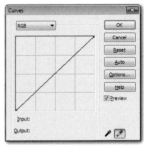

The histogram showed us how pixel lightness values are presently distributed in the image; each pixel has its own current lightness value. The Curves adjustment lets us tell various pixels to change these 'before' (**Input**) lightness values to 'after' (**Output**) values. By operating in this way on different sections of the lightness distribution, we can create a new lightness distribution more to our liking.

Let's begin at the low end. In our image, there were no pixels with a **Level** value below 63. Since we want a true black (or 0 level) in the image, we need to tell that single pixel with **Input** lightness of **63** to change to an **Output** value of **0**.

17 Click the node at the bottom of the line curve and drag it to the right until the **Input** value says **63**, or your lowest **Level** value. The **Output** value should remain at **0**.

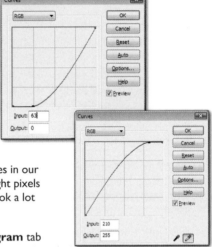

Now, to take care of the highlights, drag the topmost node to the left until the **Input** value matches the lightest pixel **Level** (**210** in our image). Again leave the **Output** unchanged, at **255**.

Click **OK**.

We've just 'spread' the dark and light values in our image, by making dark pixels darker and light pixels lighter! At this point, your image should look a lot better.

18 To confirm the result, examine the **Histogram** tab again. As you can see, the lightness values are now spread out across a much greater range, although pixels at the low and high end are still rather sparse.

Whether to make further Curves adjustments depends on how satisfied you are with the image as it stands. Simply by clicking on the Input-Output line, you can add a new node and adjust it individually, thus achieving fine control over different tonal regions of the image.

19 Open the **Curves** dialog again and click on the line to place nodes near the top and bottom. Drag the nodes slightly to create a gentle S-shaped curve as illustrated.

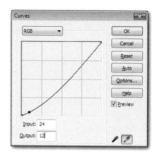

Notice how this immediately adds 'snap' to the image.

Click **Cancel** to close the dialog without applying any changes.

At this point, our sample image is satisfactory and we won't tweak its lightness levels any further. However, we'll conclude with one improvement that will benefit almost any photo.

20 On the **Effects** menu, click **Sharpen**, and then click **Unsharp Mask**.

21 In the **Filter Gallery** dialog:

- Set the **Radius** value to **2** pixels.

- Leave the **Amount** at **50%** and the **Threshold** at **0**.

- Click **OK**.

22 Repeat steps 20 and 21 using the same settings.

You should now have a sharp, tonally corrected image.

The **Unsharp Mask** function improves image quality by accentuating differences primarily at edges within the image.

You can adjust the amount of sharpening, the radius or distance from the edge, and the threshold before the filter is applied. (Use a higher setting if the image is grainy, so you don't amplify the grain.)

As a rule, run **Unsharp Mask** as the last step in an editing sequence, so as not to produce artefacts that other operations might worsen. You'll get better results running the function twice at a lower setting than running it once at a high setting.

Making Contrast Adjustments

Learn about the various methods you can increase the contrast in a photograph.

In this tutorial, you'll work with the following:

- Brightness/Contrast adjustments

- Unsharp Mask filter

- Shadow/Highlight/Midtone adjustments

Although all of the image adjustments made in this exercise can be applied directly to an image, for best practice we'll be using **adjustment layers** and **filter layers**.

Adjustment layers and filter layers provide more flexibility and let you apply changes experimentally without affecting your original image. You can turn these layers on and off to compare 'before' and 'after' images, and can also easily edit and delete them later.

Making Contrast Adjustments

Contrast adjustment can be achieved in several ways. This tutorial discusses the various methods available, comparing each one's merits along the way.

1 On the **File** menu, click **Open** (or from the Startup Wizard, select **open saved work**). Browse to the **Tutorials\Workspace** folder and open the **Cat.png** file. In a standard installation, you'll find this in the following location:

C:\Program Files\Serif\PhotoPlus\X2\Tutorials\Workspace

2 On the **Layers** tab, click  **New Adjustment Layer**. In the adjustments list, choose **Brightness/Contrast**.

In the **Brightness/Contrast** dialog, select the **Preview** check box, and then gradually drag the **Contrast** slider to the right.

Watch the area of white fur on the cat's chest. A contrast increase level of 10 is about as much as you can get away with (near right). Much more than that and the fur looks burnt out (far right).

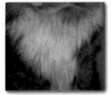

We have, however, only considered one part of the image. A contrast increase of 10 does not do a lot for the background of the image. To bring the background out, we need a much greater contrast increase, but that would result in an undesirable effect on the cat's fur.

In this case, this tool is not powerful enough to give the control needed.

3 Click **Cancel** to close the **Brightness/Contrast** dialog.

4 On the **Layers** tab, right-click on the Background layer and choose **Convert to Filter Layer**.

In the **Filter Gallery**, expand the **Sharpen** category and click the **Unsharp Mask** swatch.

Enter the following values:

- **Amount** 20
- **Radius** 50
- **Threshold** 0

Click **OK**.

Making Contrast Adjustments

What you have achieved here is a local contrast enhancement.

Although the result is still quite subtle, there is a definite improvement in image quality.

before

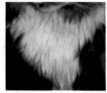

after

Note especially that the detail in the background has been brought out, without over-exposing the white chest fur.

When you have finished experimenting, press **Ctrl+Z** to undo the changes.

5 On the **Image** menu, click **Adjust**, then **Shadow/Highlight/Midtone**.

This adjustment provides a powerful way to manipulate the contrast of an image. You can effectively make the shadows in an image lighter, and the highlights in an image darker. Let's try it...

6 In the **Filter Gallery** dialog, in the lower left View drop-down list, select 200%.

The cat's chest should now be in view in the Preview window. (If it's not, adjust it by clicking on the image preview and dragging with the Pan cursor.)

On the View toolbar, click the Vertical split-screen button.

In the **Shadows** section:

- Reduce the value for **Intensity** to **0**.

- Now slowly begin to increase it back up towards **50**. Notice that as you do so, the shadows in the image become lighter.

> Increasing the **Range** value simply makes the operation act on a greater number of pixels, (thus increasing the overall effect).
>
> Increasing the **Radius** makes PhotoPlus look at a greater number of pixels around the one being changed to determine if it is a shadow or not.

Making Contrast Adjustments

The **Highlights** section of the dialog allows us to darken the highlights of an image. In this case, increasing the **Intensity** value, will darken the light parts of the image.

Note that when manipulating either the shadows or the highlights, it is usually best to only adjust one at a time.

For this reason, before proceeding to the next step, ensure that all three sliders are set to **0** in the **Shadows** section.

7 In the **Highlights** section, set the **Range** and **Radius** values to **50** and **25** respectively, then increase the **Intensity** to **50**.

The difference is clear to see on the white fur of the cat's chest

Increasing the intensity further will darken the fur until it is almost brown, but will also darken the background of the image to an unnatural extent.

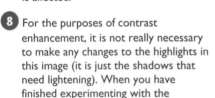

before   after

To remedy this, we could reduce the **Radius** value so less of the background is affected.

> Although not necessary for this example, we could also adjust the midtone contrast with the **Contrast** slider. This adjustment would only act on the grey tones in the image, instead of all tones.

8 For the purposes of contrast enhancement, it is not really necessary to make any changes to the highlights in this image (it is just the shadows that need lightening). When you have finished experimenting with the **Highlights** section, set all three sliders back to **0**.

In the **Shadows** section, enter **Intensity**, **Range**, and **Radius** values of **40**, **40**, and **30**. Click **OK**.

In our final image, notice that the shadows have become lighter, without any detrimental effect to the light areas of the image.

A lot of work has been done to achieve quite subtle results. However, the human eye is very acute to small-scale adjustments such as those carried out here. We think that when you view the images side by side, you will appreciate the improvements.

> Which technique you choose depends on the image you are working on. You may find that the **Brightness/Contrast** adjustment tool works just fine. If not, you have now experimented with some of the other powerful techniques available in PhotoPlus.

Creating Macros and Batch Processing

Suppose you have a set of photographs that you would like to share with your family or friends. Chances are that they are either too big, occupy too much disk space, or are the wrong file format.

In this tutorial we will show you how PhotoPlus's macro and batch processing capabilities can be combined to easily solve problems such as these.

In this tutorial, you will learn how to:

- Resize an image quickly and easily using a macro.

- Use batch processing to apply your macro to multiple images.

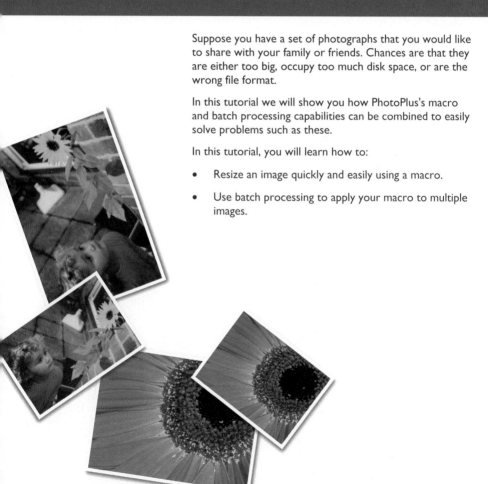

Macros and Batch Processing

Before we start this exercise, let's take some time out to explain exactly what we mean by 'macro.'

A macro is simply a saved sequence of steps (for example, commands, keyboard strokes, or mouse clicks) that you can store and then recall later with a single command or keyboard stroke. Macros are particularly useful for multi-step tasks that are carried out repeatedly, or complex procedures that are time consuming to reproduce—simply record the steps once, then replay the recording whenever you like.

1 Now we know what a macro is, let's create one...

- Click the **Macros** tab. If you can't see the tab, click **View**, choose **View Tabs**, and then select **Macros Tab**.

- On the **Macros** tab, click 📁 **New Category**. In the **Category** dialog, in the **Name** box, type 'My Macros.' Click **OK**.

- In the **Macros** tab category list, ensure that **My Macros** is the selected category, and then click the ⊞ **New Macro** button. In the **New Macro** dialog, enter the name for the macro as 'My Resize.' Click **OK**.

  You have just created the **My Resize** macro in the **My Macros** category. Your **Macros** tab should now look like ours.

2 Now that we have our category and empty macro set up, we can start recording our macro steps.

We want our macro to help us resize images, so we will need to record specific values in the **Image Size** dialog.

Most of PhotoPlus' functionality is available only with an open image. Therefore, before we can record a macro, we need to open an image.

> 💡 When creating macros, it's worthwhile jotting down on paper what you want to record in your macro **before** you actually begin recording. This will save a lot of potential mistakes. As a final note, it doesn't matter how long you take carrying out the steps you are recording; PhotoPlus will record only the commands carried out, not the time taken to do so.

3 On the **File** menu, click **New** and create a new image of default dimensions.

On the **Macros** tab, with the **My Resize** macro selected, click the ⊙ **Start Recording** button.

Creating Macros and Batch Processing

4 On the **Image** menu, select **Image Size**. In the **Image Size** dialog:

- Select the **Resize Layers** and **Maintain aspect ratio** check boxes.
- In the **Pixel Size** section, change the units to **percent**, and enter both the **Width** and **Height** as **50**.
- Click **OK**.

5 That is all we need to record, so back on the **Macros** tab, click ☐ **Stop Recording**.

Note: You must click **Stop Recording** when you have finished performing all the steps you want in your macro, otherwise you will be adding actions to it that you may not want!

○ We used the default resampling method for our macro example, but you might want to adjust this depending on the image quality required for your resulting images.

At this point, you may be thinking that since we had to enter settings into a dialog, each time we run the macro, that same dialog will be displayed and will require input. This does not have to be the case, as we'll now show you.

6 On the **Macros** tab, click the arrow to the left of **My Resize**.

This expands the macro to show each of the constituent steps included. In our case we have just the one step, automatically labelled **Image Size** due to displaying the **Image Size** dialog.

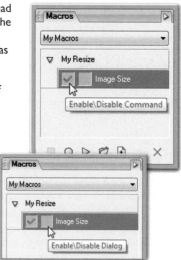

Here, we can enable or disable constituent steps in the dialog by adding or removing a check mark: you will see that **Image Size** is enabled by default in our macro.

We can also choose whether to show any dialog that may be associated with a constituent step. The default (and the best option here) is to not show the dialog each time the macro is run; you can change this if desired by clicking to add or remove the check mark.

Now we have our macro, let's test it.

Creating Macros and Batch Processing

7 Click **File**, then **Open**. Browse to your **Tutorials\Workspace** folder and open the **Sunflower.png** file. In a default installation, you'll find this folder in the following location:

C:\Program Files\Serif\PhotoPlus\X2\Tutorials\Workspace

This image is not ridiculously big, but our macro will make both viewing and electronic transfer of the image easier.

8 On the **Macros** tab, ensure **My Resize** is the selected macro, then click the ▷ **Play** button. Instantly, the image is resized to 50% of its original dimensions, and will now only occupy roughly half the disk space when saved.

Although this macro works perfectly well on individual images, the real power of it is not exposed until it is used in conjunction with batch processing. Batch processing gives us the capability to process several images in a similar way, all in one step. In our case, we would like to be able to apply our macro to several images that all need resizing. PhotoPlus provides a method to do just that!

9 On the **File** menu, select **Batch**.

The **Batch** dialog lets us use a macro in the batch process if required, which is just what we want. We can also specify the output file type, the folder that contains all the images to be processed, and the folder that is to contain all the processed images.

10 In the **Batch** dialog:

- Select the **Use Macro** check box.
- In the **Category** drop-down list, select **My Macros**.
- In the **Macro** list, select **My Resize** (currently the only macro in the list).
- Select the **Change File Type** check box, and select **JPEG** as the format.
- In the **Source Folder** section, click **Browse** and then browse to a folder containing images you want to resize. (If you don't have your own images, use the **Tutorials\Workspace** folder.)
  Select the folder and then click **OK**.
- In the **Destination** section, click **Browse**. Create a new folder in a convenient location, say **C:\Resized Images**.
- At the bottom of the dialog, click **Modify**.

The **File Name Format** dialog opens. Here, we can specify how each processed file is to be labelled.

Creating Macros and Batch Processing

11 In the **Tokens** pane, select **Document Name** and then click **Add**.

- Select **Text** and then click **Add**. A **Text** box displays beneath the **Format** pane. In the box, type '_small.' This ensures that each processed image will have a filename consisting of its original filename, followed by **_small**.

- Click **OK** to close the **File Name Format** dialog.

12 Back in the **Batch** dialog, all our settings are complete, so click **OK** to run the batch process.

You will see PhotoPlus open each image in the specified source folder, apply the macro, and then close the image.

13 Browse to the folder you specified as your destination folder. You will see that all the images there have been reduced in dimensions by 50%, and are now JPG in format.

Compare the time taken to apply this batch process with how long it would take to open each image, display the **Image Size** dialog, specify the new dimensions, and then export the image as a JPG.

To resize multiple images at best quality (Lanczos3 Window), you can also use the new **Resize Image** functionality now included in the **Batch** dialog.

To simply resize images:

1. Clear the **Use Macro** checkbox and adjust the settings in the **Resize Images** section.
2. Choose your source and destination folders.
3. Specify file type and file name if required.
4. Click **OK**.

- or -

To run a macro and also resize images:

1. Select the **Use Macro** checkbox.
2. Select the macro category and name from the drop-down lists.
3. Adjust the settings in the **Resize Images** section.
4. Choose your source and destination folders.
5. Specify file type and file name if required.
6. Click **OK**.

Creating Macros and Batch Processing

This tutorial has focused on combining a custom macro with a batch process to resize a collection of images.

However, the **Macros** tab provides an extensive selection of predefined macros. With these you can quickly and easily enhance, manipulate, and apply creative effects to a single image, or, when used in a batch process, to multiple images.

In the example on the right, we applied a dreamy black and white effect with the **Black & White Photography** category's **Infrared** macro.

For more information on macros, see the *PhotoPlus User Guide* or online Help.

Creative Effects

If you're keen to work on something a little different, choose one of these tutorials and learn how to create an original work of art.

- **Antiquing Photographs**
- **Combining Depth Maps and 3D Effects**
- **Creating Dramatic Lighting Effects**
- **Creating Oil Painting Effects**
- **Using Paths**
- **Creating Modern Art**
- **Working With Vector Shapes**
- **Creating Infrared Effects**

Antiquing Photographs

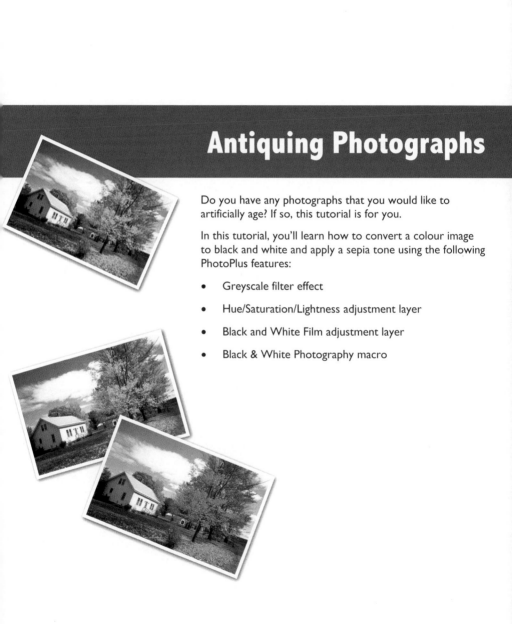

Do you have any photographs that you would like to artificially age? If so, this tutorial is for you.

In this tutorial, you'll learn how to convert a colour image to black and white and apply a sepia tone using the following PhotoPlus features:

- Greyscale filter effect

- Hue/Saturation/Lightness adjustment layer

- Black and White Film adjustment layer

- Black & White Photography macro

Antiquing Photographs

In the following exercise, we've taken a recent colour photograph of a house, and given it an 'antiqued' effect. You'll probably want to try this with one of your own images. If you don't have one, however, you can use our sample file—**House.jpg**.

In a standard installation, you'll find this file in the following location:

C:\Program Files\Serif\PhotoPlus\X2\Tutorials\Workspace

1 Open PhotoPlus. Click **File**, then **Open** and open the image you want to use.

2 On the **Image** menu, choose **Adjust**, and then select **Greyscale**.

3 The **Filter Gallery** opens. In the Preview pane the image displays with the greyscale filter applied.

The Greyscale filter sliders provide fine control over the level of Red, Green and Blue in a greyscale image.

4 Adjust the values as follows:

Red 15

Green 50

Blue 15

This balances all three channels out to be roughly equal.

Click **OK** and view the result.

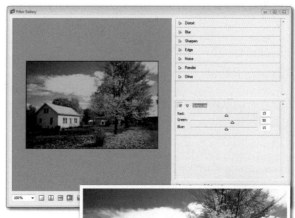

> Experiment with various combinations of the three colour channels. Be aware, however, that as a general rule the values should add up to roughly 100, or the result will be somewhat un-natural.

As you can see, converting an image to greyscale does give an aged effect to photographs (whatever method you use), but for a more complete effect, a sepia tone is required.

7 Click **Ctrl+Z** to revert to the original full colour image.

8 On the **Image** menu, choose **Adjust** and then select **Hue/Saturation/Lightness**.

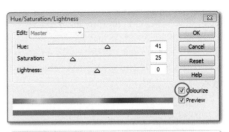

9 In the **Hue/Saturation/Lightness** dialog:

- Select the **Colourize** check box.
- Adjust the **Hue** to **41**.
- Click **OK**.

This simple technique may well be sufficient for your needs, but should you require greater control over the various colour channels in your image, you can do so with a **Black and White Film adjustment**.

This adjustment converts a colour image to black and white with intelligent control over grey tones of up to seven colours. Additionally the adjustment offers a simple way of applying a colour tint. Let's try this now...

10 Click **Ctrl+Z** to revert to the original full colour image once more.

11 On the **Layers** tab, click ▨ **New Adjustment Layer** and select **Black and White Film**.

12 In the **Black and White Film** dialog:

- Drag the sliders left or right to darken or lighten the grey tones of the original image.
- For colour tinting effects, select the **Tint** check box and then drag the **Hue** slider to achieve the required tint. Drag the **Saturation** slider to adjust tint intensity.

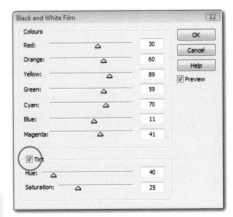

13 Click **OK** to apply the adjustment, or **Cancel** to abandon changes.

For portraits, adjusting the sensitivity to **Orange** will affect skin tones.

Antiquing Photographs

Using PhotoPlus macros

PhotoPlus also provides a range of preset Black & White Photography macros, which you can use to apply various greyscale effects to an image with a single-click.

To run a black and white macro:

1 On the **Macros** tab, select **Black & White Photography** from the drop-down list of categories.

2 Select the macro you want to run, and then click ▷ **Play**.

Original   Infrared (Dreamy)   Orange Filter

The methods described in this tutorial can be used to apply a wide range of 'antique' effects to your photos. Which method you use depends on the image you are working on, and the effect you are aiming to achieve.

To achieve the best results, we suggest that you experiment with various techniques and settings as you work on your own projects.

Combining Depth Maps with 3D Effects

Add a convincing 'touch' to an image using a depth map and a 3D effect.

In this tutorial, you will:

- Create a new image.

- Use the Colour tab and Flood Fill tool to apply colour.

- Use the Layer Effects dialog to apply 3D Depth and Lighting effects.

- Make selections.

- Copy and paste images.

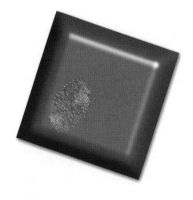

Combining Depth Maps with 3D Effects

Combining Depth Maps with 3D Effects

This relatively simple tutorial offers an interesting application for a depth map and a basic 3D effect. The 3D Lighting controls come into play this time, too.

1 Open PhotoPlus and from the Startup Wizard, select **create new picture** (if PhotoPlus is already open, click **File**, then **New**) .

In the **New Image** dialog, set the **Width** and **Height** to **400** pixels, and the **Background** to **Transparent**. Click **OK**.

2 On the **Colour** tab, set the **Colour Mode** to RGB. In the upper left corner of the tab, click the foreground colour swatch and set its colour to **RGB (87, 43, 16)**.

Note: If the foreground colour swatch was already selected when you clicked it, the **Adjust Colour** dialog will open—set your RGB values there and click **OK**.

3 On the Tools toolbar, on the Fill tools flyout, click the ⬥ **Flood Fill** tool, then click inside your blank image to fill it with the brown colour we've specified.

It doesn't look fantastic yet, but don't worry there's more to come!

4 On the **Layers** tab, click ⚡ **Add Layer Effects** to open the **Layer Effects** dialog.

5 In the **Effects** list, select the **3D Effects** check box:

- Adjust the **Blur** to **65** and the **Depth** to **270**.

6 Click the **3D Lighting** effect. In the **Light Properties** section:

- Change the **Angle** to **56** and the **Elevation** to **61**.

- Adjust the **Soften** value to **10**. (This will blur the highlights introduced by the 3D Lighting.)

- Click **OK**.

We now need to prepare our image for more effects.

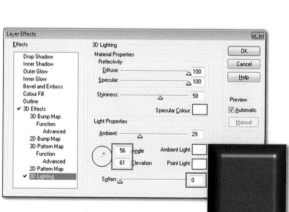

Combining Depth Maps with 3D Effects

7 On the **Layers** tab, right-click and choose **Merge All**. This 'flattens' the image and its 3D effect, allowing us to apply another effect to the same image.

> 🛈 Now that we have merged our image with its 3D effects, we can no longer edit the 3D Depth and Lighting settings—unless we use the **Edit/Undo** command or the **History** tab to retrace our steps.

8 Click **File**, then **Open**. Browse to the **Tutorials\Workspace** folder and open the **Chocolate.jpg** file. In a standard installation, you'll find this in the following location:

C:\Program Files\Serif\PhotoPlus\X2\Tutorials\Workspace

9 On the **Select** menu, choose **Select All** (or press **Ctrl+A**) to select the whole image—you'll see a dotted line appear around the image.

On the **Edit** menu, click **Copy** (or **Ctrl+C**) to copy the image to the Clipboard.

10 Close the **Chocolate.jpg** file. The original image is active again.

11 On the **Layers** tab, right-click the **Background** layer and choose **Promote to Layer**.

Click the 🔺 **Add Layer Depth Map** button, then press **Ctrl+A** to create a selection around your image.

12 On the **Edit** menu, choose **Paste**, then **Into Selection** to paste the contents of your Clipboard into the selection.

Click **Select**, then **Deselect** (**Ctrl+D**) to deselect the image.

13 On the **Layers** tab, click 🔷 **Add Layer Effects** to open the **Layer Effects dialog**.

- In the **3D Effects** section, set the **Blur** to **0** and **Depth** to **1**.

- In the **3D Lighting** section, adjust the light source angle and elevation to your liking.

  In theory these settings should be the same as those used previously, in step 6. We used the same **Angle** and **Elevation** settings (**56** and **61** respectively), but reduced the **Soften** setting to **2** for a better effect.

- Click **OK**.

Your image should resemble ours...

Creating Dramatic Lighting Effects

Bring a photo to life using lighting effects.

In this tutorial, you'll learn how to:

- Create drama in a photo by adding lighting effects.

- Manipulate light source properties to create different effects.

- Add multiple light sources.

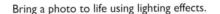

Although all of the lighting effects made in this exercise can be applied directly to your image, for best practice we'll be using **filter layers**.

Filter layers provide more flexibility and let you apply changes experimentally without affecting your original image. You can turn these layers on and off to compare 'before' and 'after' images, and can also easily edit and delete them later.

Creating Dramatic Lighting Effects

In this tutorial we'll bring a photograph to life by adding our own lighting effects.

The photograph we have chosen has very little colour in it and looks quite unexciting. We'll show you how easy it is to add colour and texture to produce the result shown.

1 On the Standard toolbar, click 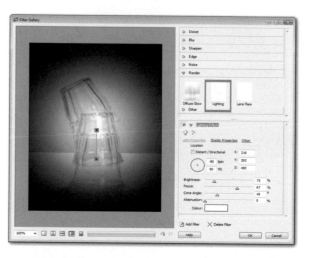 **Open**. Browse to the **Tutorials/Workspace** folder and open the **Wine Glasses.png** file. In a standard installation, you'll find this in the following location:

C:\Program Files\Serif\PhotoPlus\X2\Tutorials\Workspace

2 On the **Layers** tab, right-click the Background layer and click **Convert to Filter Layer**.

3 In the **Filter Gallery**, click the **Render** category and then click the **Lighting** swatch.

In the **Lighting Effects** section of the dialog, you can access the **Light Properties**, **Shader Properties**, and **Other** properties by clicking their respective headings.

We want to create a soft vignette around the subject to draw attention to it. We can do this by adding a spotlight effect.

4 There should already be a light source at the centre of the page (two black squares joined by a dotted line). The handles of the light source control the position and size of the spotlight. Drag the handles so the light frames the wine glasses (the **Spin** value should be approximately -90).

5 Adjust the **Brightness**, **Focus**, and **Cone Angle** values to fine tune the shape and strength of the light until you're happy with the result. We used the following values:

Spin:	-90
Tilt:	90
Brightness:	75%
Focus:	67
Cone Angle:	45°
Attenuation:	0%
Colour: White (RGB 255, 255, 255)	

Creating Dramatic Lighting Effects

We'll now adjust the shade by controlling the ambient light and its colour, the diffuse light, and the specular (directly reflected) light and its colour.

6 Click **Shader Properties** and enter the following values:

Ambient:	30
Diffuse:	95
Specular:	85
Shininess:	86
Ambient Colour:	RGB (51, 153, 204)
Specular Colour:	RGB (102, 102, 255)

7 To emphasize the shape of the wine glasses and make them stand out more, let's add some texture. Click **Other** and enter the following values:

Texture Channel:	Luminance
Blur:	2
Depth:	20

8 When you're happy with your results, click **OK**.

9 If you now save this new image as a PhotoPlus .SPP file, you'll be able to edit the Lighting Effects settings later by simply double-clicking on the filter layer to reopen the **Filter Gallery**.

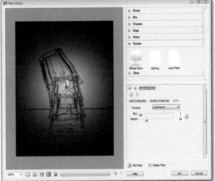

Multiple Light Sources

In this example we'll use three different coloured light sources pointing in different directions to create a more striking image: a red one in the upper right corner pointing towards the opposite corner; a blue one in the lower left corner pointing towards the middle right area, creating a coloured gradient across the image; and finally a white light source at the centre to highlight the centre of the image and create a focal point.

You can add extra light sources using the button, positioned in the top left corner of the right **Filter Properties** pane.

(In principle, you can add as many light sources as you like and you'll have full control over the properties of each one individually.)

1 Open the original **Wine Glasses.png** file. Repeat steps 2 and 3 of the previous section to add a **Lighting Effects** filter layer.

Creating Dramatic Lighting Effects

2 Drag the first light source into the upper right corner of the preview pane, as illustrated and set the following values:

Spin:	-133
Tilt:	60
Brightness:	100
Focus:	75
Cone Angle:	60°
Attenuation:	0%
Colour:	RGB (128, 0, 0)

3 Click the 💡 button to add another light source, then click on the image in the preview pane to position the light source in the lower left area — you can 'fine tune' it later. The values we used are provided below:

Spin:	15
Tilt:	90
Brightness:	75
Focus:	60
Cone Angle:	45°
Attenuation:	0%
Colour:	RGB (0, 0, 128)

4 Add a third light source, roughly in the centre of the image, with the following settings:

Spin:	35
Tilt:	90
Brightness:	75
Focus:	50
Cone Angle:	35°
Attenuation:	0%
Colour: White (RGB 255, 255, 255)	

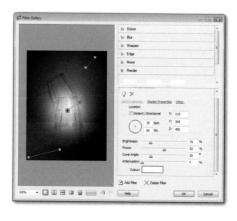

5 Now add a logo and a slogan (in PhotoPlus or PagePlus) to turn the photograph into a striking advertisement.

The final advert could look something like this:

Creating an Oil Painting Effect

Create a striking oil painting effect by applying an Instant Artist effect.

In this tutorial, you'll learn how to:

- Apply an Instant Artist effect.

- Add a layer depth map.

- Apply and adjust 3D lighting effects.

Creating an Oil Painting Effect

The PhotoPlus Instant Artist effects let you quickly and easily transform your images to simulate various styles of painting. In this exercise, we'll create a striking oil painting effect by further enhancing the result of Instant Artist effects.

1 To get started, run PhotoPlus and click **File**, then **Open** (or from the Startup Wizard click **open saved work**). Browse to the **Tutorials\Workspace** folder, and open the **Farmhouse.jpg** file. In a standard installation, you'll find this in the following location:

C:\Program Files\Serif\PhotoPlus\X2\Tutorials\Workspace

2 On the **Effects** menu, select **Instant Artist**. In the **Instant Artist** dialog:

- Select the **Oil** effect.
- Change the **Brush Size** setting to **8**.
- Change the **Weight** setting to **20**.
- Change the **Max Length** setting to **20**.
- Change the **Blur** setting to **10**.
- Change the **Enhance** setting to **High**.
- Click **OK**.

🔋 After you click **OK**, it's normal for there to be a processing delay while PhotoPlus applies the effect.

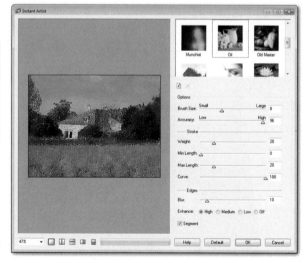

Let's now give the 'brush strokes' some depth in the surface of the paint.

3 On the **Edit** menu, click **Copy (Ctrl+C)** to copy the image to your Clipboard.

On the **Layers** tab, right-click the **Background** layer and choose **Promote to Layer**.

The layer is renamed 'Layer 1.'

4 On the **Layers** tab, click the 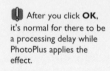 **Add Layer Depth Map** button.

Creating an Oil Painting Effect

5 On the **Select** menu, click **Select All (Ctrl+A)** to create a selection around your image.

Click **Edit** and choose **Paste**, then **Into Selection (Shift+Ctrl+L)** to paste the contents of your Clipboard into the selection on the depth map.

This has created a depth map, introducing light and shadow to 'high' and 'low' parts of the image derived from light and dark areas of the original 'oil painted' image.

Adding a depth map to an image automatically activates the standard **3D Layer** effect with default settings. At the moment, the image has some quite heavy 'embossing' so we'll need to alter the 3D settings to achieve the effect we're after.

6 On the **Layers** tab, click the 🗲 **Layer Effects** button.

In the **Layer Effects** dialog, in the **Effects** list, select **3D Effects**.

- Change the **Blur** to **2**.
- Change the **Depth** to **4**.

7 Now select the **3D Lighting** section.

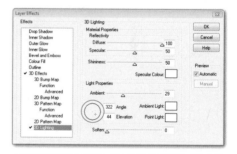

- Adjust both the **Specular** and **Shininess** settings to **50**.

- Experiment with the **Angle** and **Elevation** of the light source for best results. To do this, simply drag the red cross-hair inside the circle.

- When you're happy with your results, click **OK**.

> ❗ The **Specular** setting controls how bright the highlights are, and the **Shininess** adjusts the overall handling of light across the effect.

That's all there is to it. In a few steps, we've applied an Instant Artist effect, added some relief to our brush strokes using a depth map, and added 3D lighting effects.

You can modify the light settings further, and experiment with different Instant Artist settings to suit your taste.

Using Paths

Create a unique path and learn a handy application for paths: converting to a selection.

In this tutorial, you'll learn how to:

- Create a new path.

- Use the Curved Outline tool.

- Use the Node Edit tool.

- Convert a path to a selection.

Using Paths

In this tutorial, you'll see how useful it can be to create an editable selection outline using the **Path** tool. We'll start by creating a unique curved path, then explore converting the path to a selection. You can use your own image for this exercise, or you can use our sample image, **Duck.jpg**, located in the **Tutorials\Workspace folder.**

In a default installation, you'll find this folder in the following location:

C:\Program Files\Serif\PhotoPlus\X2\Tutorials\Workspace

1 Open PhotoPlus, then on the **File** menu, click **Open**. Browse to the **Tutorials\Workspace** folder and open the **Duck.jpg** file.

This image shows a bath time duck on a relatively uniform background. You could, of course, use the **Colour Selection** tool or the **Extract** tool to remove the background but we'd like to show you the power and flexibility of the Curved Outline tool for such simple shapes.

The main advantages of the **Curved Outline** tool are as follows:

*   You have ultimate control over the exact shape of the outline created.

*   You can adjust the outline at any time.

*   You can save the outline as a 'path' in the document.

2 On the **Layers** tab list, right-click on the **Background** layer, and select **Promote to Layer**. The layer is now renamed **Layer 1**. (You can rename the layer yourself by double-clicking it on the **Layers** tab to open the **Layer Properties** dialog.)

3 On the Line tools flyout, select the Curved Outline tool.

4 On the Context toolbar, select the Paths button, then click a point around the duck to begin: we started just under the duck's bill and continued clockwise. This is the start of our curve path.

If you click and drag, 'curve handles' extend from the node you've just created. You can also move the curve handles to alter the shape of the curve.

Using Paths

This 'drag to define' curve handle length is something you should experiment with.

Long curve handles make for gentle curvature of your path at and to either side of the point clicked.

Short curve handles allow for tighter curves. Don't worry if your curves are inaccurate; they can be easily edited once your curve is finished.

For more information, see online Help.

5 Continue clicking and dragging at places around the duck where the curve changes direction. Try to follow the shape as closely as possible.

6 On the **Paths** tab, right-click the new path and choose **Rename Path**. In the **Path Name** dialog, name your new path 'Outline.'

(Although we'll only have one path in this document, naming appropriately is a good habit to adopt.)

We have created ten nodes around the duck, see illustration, left. (the numbers have been added to show the order of the nodes; node no. 9 is selected).

A similar curve could probably have been made with less nodes. Fewer nodes should mean smoother curves, but it's sometimes easier and quicker to create the necessary changes in direction by adding nodes more frequently.

7 When you reach the start of your path, close the path (join the two ends) by clicking on the first node (numbered **1** in our illustration, above); a small square will appear on the cursor to indicate that the curve will be closed if you click at this point.

8 If necessary, you can edit your curve to improve it. You can 'tweak' the outline by moving the nodes and/or dragging the 'curve handles' using the **Node Edit** tool.

Using Paths

You can use the buttons on the Context toolbar to change the selected node type from **Symmetric** to **Sharp** or **Smooth** for fine control. Each type's control handles behave a bit differently, as you will find out after a bit of experimentation.

For more information, see "Drawing and Editing Lines and Shapes" in online Help.

To edit the curve:

- On the Tools toolbar, on the Shape Edit tool flyout, select the 🖘 **Node Edit** tool.

- Click a node to select it, and then click and drag the outlying handles to modify the curve either side of the node

  - or -

  Click and drag the curve itself to reshape curve segments.

9 When you've finished editing your path outline, save your image as a PhotoPlus .SPP file to retain the path for future editing.

10 On the **Paths** tab, click the ▢ **Path to Selection** button at the bottom of the tab. Set the **Feather** to **0** and click **OK**.

If your selection is slightly too large or too small, you can choose **Select,** then **Modify**, then **Contract** or **Expand** to reduce or enlarge the size of the selection.

11 On the **Select** menu, choose **Invert**, then press the **Delete** key. The background disappears.

12 Click **Select**, then choose **Deselect** (or press **Ctrl+D**) to clear the selection.

In summary, you have 'cut' the duck out of the original photograph by creating a path using the **Curve Outline** tool—a simple elegant method. The cut-out can now be pasted into any image you like, or even turned into a PhotoPlus Brush.

Creating Modern Art

With a few strokes of the Gradient Fill tool and the use of different blend modes you can easily create abstract works of art from scratch.

In this tutorial, you will:

- Use the Gradient Fill tool.

- Use the Context toolbar to adjust blend mode, opacity, gradient fill and gradient style settings.

- Apply a Gaussian Blur effect.

- Adjust hue.

Modern Art

In this tutorial, we'll show you how easy it is to create a modern art composition in just a few simple steps.

1 Open a new document. This example uses an image size of **10** × **10** cm at a resolution of **300** dpi.

2 On the Tools toolbar, select the ▨ **Gradient Fill** tool (located on the Fill tools flyout).

The Context toolbar for this tool automatically opens: check the that **Blend Mode** is **Normal**, the **Opacity** is **100%** and the **Gradient** type is **Linear**.

Click the Gradient box.

In the **Gradient** dialog, choose one of the multicoloured gradients, or create your own.

On the Context toolbar, leave **Reverse** cleared and **Transparency** selected for the time being — you can experiment with these later to see their effects.

3 To begin, draw a short horizontal line across the middle page to create a series of coloured vertical bands similar to our illustration.

If you leave the Blend Mode as **Normal** then each gradient fill you consequently draw will replace what you have already drawn; however, by changing the blend mode you can combine the newly drawn gradient fills with the existing ones to create some interesting and artistic effects. You'll find a summary of the various Blend Modes in Chapter 5 of the *PhotoPlus Resource Guide*.

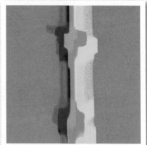

4 For example, change the Blend Mode to **Overlay** (to combine highlights and shadows from the underlying image with the main colours and patterns from the tool stroke). Reduce opacity to reduce the effect of the tool stroke on the underlying image. An Opacity value of **75%** was used in this example. Now use the Gradient Fill tool to draw some short vertical lines in the striped section of your image.

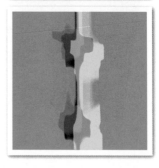

5 Now draw a couple of diagonal lines through the original coloured bands. Repeat this in the other direction.

Creating Modern Art

6 Increase this 'whittling' effect by drawing a couple of broad horizontal strokes across the image. (This makes the colours more solid).

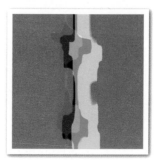

7 To create the final image (above), we blurred the image slightly and changed the hue:

- Click **Effects**, then **Blur**, then **Gaussian Blur**. Change the **Radius** value to 5.

- Click **Image**, then **Adjust**, then **Hue/Saturation/Lightness**. Change the **Hue** to **90**.

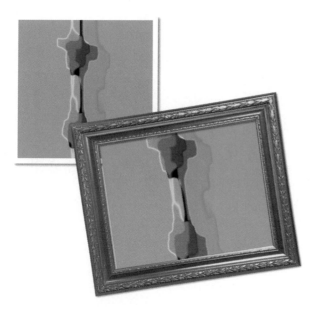

Feel free to experiment with other types of Gradient Fill types (Linear, Radial, Conical, or Square). Try changing the Opacity, Gradient, and Blend Modes—the possibilities are endless!

The following pages contain other examples to inspire you.

Creating Modern Art

Other Examples

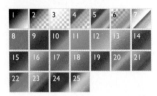

Gradient Chart

This chart illustrates the standard Gradients available. A number has been assigned to each Gradient and is referred to in these examples.

Pointillist Sunset

Settings used
Blend Mode Dissolve
Opacity   10%
Gradient   23
Gradient Style: Conical
Reverse   Off
Transparency: On

Crossed Polaroids

Settings used
Blend Mode Difference
Opacity   75%
Gradient   5
Gradient Style: Linear
Reverse   No
Transparency: Yes

Creating Modern Art

Squares

Dark Rain

Initially fill the background with the Blend Mode set to Normal then use the settings below.

Settings used
Blend Mode Soft Light
Opacity   60%
Gradient   20
Gradient Style: Linear
Reverse   Yes
Transparency: Yes

Settings used
Blend Mode Difference
Opacity   50%
Gradient   9
Gradient Style: Square
Reverse   Off
Transparency: On

Silk

Cubist

Initially fill the background with the Blend Mode then go crazy with the mouse lots of small blends

Settings used
Blend Mode Difference
Opacity   100%
Gradient   1
Gradient Style: Linear
Reverse   Off
Transparency: Yes

With the last image now as a starting point simple go crazy again with the mouse, over and over.

Settings used
Blend Mode Difference
Opacity   100%
Gradient   7
Gradient Style: Linear
Reverse   Off
Transparency: Yes

Working With Vector Shapes

Add editable vector shapes to a photograph, and then apply gradient fills and transparency to create a realistic landscape scene.

In this tutorial, you'll learn how to:

- Use layers to combine two existing images.

- Create and edit vector shapes.

- Apply and adjust gradient fills with the Gradient Fill tool.

- Apply transparency to a shape.

- Work with the Colour Pickup, Colour Selection, Deform, and Clone tools.

- Add and link layers and work with layer masks.

Working With Vector Shapes

In this tutorial, we'll start with two existing photos—one depicting a desert landscape; the other the moon against a black background. We'll combine these images and then add our own vector shapes to create a dramatic, but realistic effect. You can, of course, apply the same techniques to your own images. However, we suggest you use our sample images for this exercise. You'll find the images in your **Tutorials\Workspace** folder.

In a standard installation, this folder is installed to the following location:

C:\Program Files\Serif\PhotoPlus\X2\Tutorials\Workspace

1 Open PhotoPlus. On the **File** menu, click **Open**, browse to **Tutorials/Workspace** folder and open the **Moon.jpg** file.

2 On the Tools toolbar, click the ✎ **Colour Selection** tool. On the Context toolbar, set the **Tolerance** to **100**.

3 Click on the black background area to select it, then on the **Select** menu, click **Invert**.

4 On the **Edit** menu, click **Copy** to copy to the Clipboard. Close the **Moon.jpg** file.

5 On the **File** menu, click **Open**, browse to **Tutorials/Workspace** folder and open the **Panorama.jpg** file.

6 On the **Edit** menu, choose **Paste**, then **As New Layer**, to paste the moon into this image as a new layer (named 'Layer 1' on the **Layers** tab).

7 On the Tools toolbar, select the ⬚ **Deform** tool. Then press and hold the **Shift** key and use one of the corner handles to resize the moon until is less than half of its original size.

💡Holding down the **Shift** key while dragging with the **Deform** tool constrains the shape, ensuring that our moon remains a perfect circle.

Working With Vector Shapes

8 On the Tools toolbar, click the 🖋 **Colour Pickup** tool. Click on an area of sky near the top of the image.

On the **Colour** tab, the colour you picked up should now be displayed as the new foreground colour. Click the foreground colour swatch.

In the **Adjust Colour** dialog, click **Add Custom**, and then click **OK**.

9 Repeat step 8 with a lighter colour picked from lower down in the sky.

10 Set the darker of your two new custom colours as the foreground colour. To do this:

- On the **Colour** tab, switch the foreground and background swatch colours by clicking the small arrow to the right of the swatches.

  - or -

- On the **Colour** tab, click the foreground swatch to reopen the **Adjust Colour** dialog, and then select your custom colour from the lower swatches pane.

11 On the Tools toolbar, on the QuickShapes flyout, select the **Moon**.

On the Context toolbar, ensure that **Shape Layers** is selected.

12 Now hold down the **Ctrl** key (to constrain aspect ratio) and draw a crescent moon with the same diameter as the (actual) moon.

On the Tools toolbar, select the ✛ **Move** tool, and then click and drag on the shape to move it over the left side of the moon.

13 On the Tools toolbar, on **Shape/Node Edit** flyout, select the ▶ **Node Edit** tool and then drag the Adjust node down to set the crescent moon size as in our illustration, right.

Working With Vector Shapes

14 On the same flyout, select the  **Shape Edit** tool. A square bounding box displays around the shape. Click just outside this area until you see the Rotate cursor, then rotate the shape approximately 45° anti-clockwise.

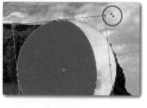

Next, we'll apply a fill and transparency to our shape.

15 On the Tools toolbar, on the Fill tools flyout, select the  **Gradient Fill** tool.

On the Context toolbar, in the Fill type drop-down list, select **Linear**, and then click the black and white Gradient Fill box.

16 In the **Gradient** dialog:

- Click to select the black node at the lower left corner of the gradient strip.

- Click the **Colour** box (currently displaying the colour black).

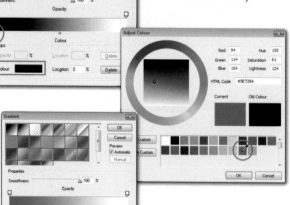

17 In the **Adjust Colour** dialog:

- Click the darker blue custom colour swatch to apply it to the gradient fill.

- Click **OK** to close the **Adjust Colour** dialog.

Back in the **Gradient** dialog, the black colour on the gradient strip has been replaced with your custom colour.

18 Now click on the white node at the lower right corner of the gradient and repeat the previous steps, this time replacing the rightmost white node with your light blue custom colour. Click **OK** to close the **Gradient** dialog.

19 On the **Layers** tab, select the layer containing your QuickShape (Layer 2), and then draw a line from top to bottom of your crescent to apply a gradient fill from dark to light blue.

Working With Vector Shapes

20 On the **Layers** tab:

- Right-click the shape layer and choose **Rasterize**.

- Click the 😊 **Add Layer Mask** button (this automatically sets your image to **Edit Mask** mode)

21 On the Context toolbar:

- Click the Gradient Fill box.

  In the **Gradient** dialog, repeat steps 15 to 18 to 'reverse' the gradient so that it graduates from the lighter to the darker blue.

  Drag the sliders so that the graduation occurs only in the rightmost section the gradient.

  Click **OK**.

- Set the **Fill** type to **Radial** and draw a gradient (length and direction shown below, right) over the moon to add transparency to the shape.

  (You might need to repeat this step to get the desired results.)

22 When you are happy with your blending, return to the **Layers** tab and link Layer 1 and Layer 2 (the layer containing the moon and the shape layer).

To link layers:

- Select the first layer, press and hold the **Ctrl** key, and then select the second layer.

- With both layers selected, right-click and choose **Link Layers**.

  Link icons now display next to the linked layers.

> Linking layers together keeps layer information together. Once layers are linked, they remain so regardless of which layer in a linked group is active.
>
> For more information, see "Manipulating Layers" in online Help.

Working With Vector Shapes

> 🔍 **An optional step:** Hide all layers but the moon layer and re-colour it using the **Hue/Saturation/Lightness** filter (click **Image**, then **Adjust**, then **Hue/Saturation/Lightness**). For instructions on using this filter, see the "Recolouring Images" tutorial.

22 Select the ✛ **Move** tool and move your linked layers into the top-right of the image.

23 On the **Layers** tab, click ⊞ **New Layer**.

In the **Layer Properties** dialog, name your new layer 'Clouds' and click **OK**.

Ensure that the new **Clouds** layer is at the top of the layer list.

24 On the Tools toolbar, select the ✐ **Clone** tool.

On the Context toolbar:

- Select the **Use All Layers** check box and clear the **Aligned** check box.
- Select a brush tip size of **25** pixels.
- Set the **Opacity** to **75**.

To define a clone source, **Shift**-click a region of cloud above the horizon.

Click to 'paint' some clouds over the moon, varying the level of opacity for more realism.

Done! Your final result should look similar to ours.

Creating Infrared Effects

Create an 'infrared' effect using an adjustment layer, a Gaussian blur, and the Channels tab.

In this tutorial, you'll learn how to:

- Duplicate layers.

- Work with the Channels tab and Channel Mixer.

- Add a blur effect from the Filter Gallery.

- Add and adjust blend modes.

Creating Infrared Effects

This tutorial aims to simulate the effect produced by infrared film. Most people are unaware that vegetation reflects a lot of infrared light, which, when captured on an infrared film, appears very bright and vivid. We demonstrate this effect here on a image of Africa.

1 Open PhotoPlus. Click **File**, then **Open** (or from the Startup Wizard click **open saved work**). Browse to the **Tutorials\Workspace** folder, and open the **Africa.jpg** file. In a standard installation, you'll find this in the following location:

C:\Program Files\Serif\PhotoPlus\X2\Tutorials\Workspace

2 On the **Layers** tab:

- Right click the **Background** layer and select **Duplicate**.

- In the **Duplicate Layer** dialog, change the default name to 'Background - green blur' (you'll see why in the next step).

- Click **OK**.

3 On the **Layers** tab, ensure that the **Background - green blur** layer is active, and then click the **Channels** tab.

The **Channels** tab allows you to view a particular colour channel—or a combination of channels—within the current image.

- Click to select the green channel.

  The green channel is now the only visible channel.

Our next step is to apply a Gaussian Blur. Since we have selected the green channel in the previous step, the effect will be applied to that channel alone.

4 On the **Effects** menu, select **Blur**, and then choose **Gaussian Blur**.

- In the **Filter Gallery**, change the **Radius** setting to **5.0** by typing into the value box or by dragging the slider.

- Click **OK**.

Creating Infrared Effects

5 On the **Channels** tab, click to select **RGB**. All four channels are now displayed.

6 On the **Layers** tab, with the **Background - green blur** layer selected:

- Change the blend mode to **Screen**.
- Adjust the **Opacity** to **5%**.

At this point you may be thinking that the result does not look too dissimilar from our initial image. What we have done, however, is take the steps necessary for our final adjustment.

7 On the **Layers** tab, click 📄 **New Adjustment Layer**, and then select **Channel Mixer**.

In the **Channel Mixer** dialog:

- Enter the values for the **Red**, **Green** and **Blue** channels as **30**, **200**, and **-70** respectively.
- Select the **Monochrome** check box.
- Click **OK** to apply the effect.

Your finished image should resemble ours, below.

Try hiding the Channel Mixer adjustment layer by clicking its eye icon to see how areas of lightness really do correspond to areas of green on the original image!

Design Projects

2

Index

Projects

This chapter contains a number of advanced creative design projects for you to try.

Index

Ink Blot

This cool effect is very easy to produce.

See how it was done...

Ink Blot

STEP 1

The first step is to give the portrait sufficient space on either side to accommodate the ink blot parts of our composition.

We convert the image to greyscale (*Image > Adjust > Greyscale*) (accept the default settings in the Filter Gallery) and use the *Levels* dialog (*Image > Adjust > Levels*) to reduce the level of detail.

Any unwanted detail is then removed using the *Standard Eraser* tool.

Original image

Levels dialog

Standard Eraser tool

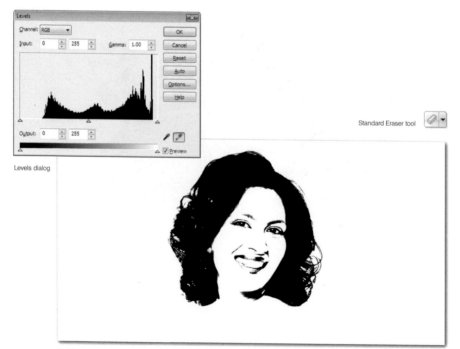

Final result

Original rose

STEP 2

The creation of the ink blot is very simple. In this case an image of a rose is inverted, using *Image > Adjust > Negative Image*.

As before the detail is reduced using the *Levels* dialog.

Final version, after negative image and levels adjustment applied

We are aiming for an abstract shape, so any organic image can be used.

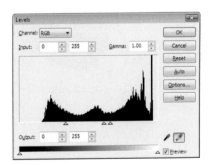

Levels dialog

Ink Blot

3

STEP 3

Using the image created from the rose, we cut parts out and rearrange the elements into a suitably attractive shape. There is no trick to this, simply go with what feels good and looks nice.

The only thing that remains is to duplicate the layer, flip it horizontally, and then merge the left side and right side into one layer.

Layers tab

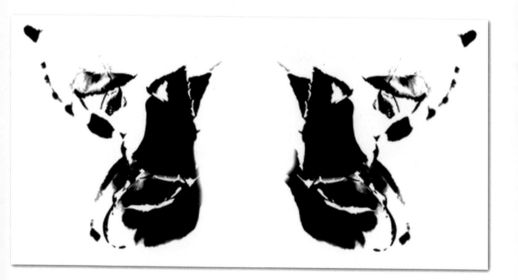

STEP 4

The final step is to simply add the ink blot to a layer above the portrait. The blend mode for this layer is set to *Multiply*.

Any extra or unwanted areas are removed with the *Standard Eraser* tool. As a final finishing touch the *Effects Grunged* brushes were used to add a few splashes of paint.

Layers tab

Eraser tool

Blots and splashes

Ink Blot

5 STEP 5

The finished image.

You could apply this effect to any photo in your collection.

Pop Art

These Pop Art images are easy to create.

See how it was done...

Pop Art

1

STEP 1 - Style 1

The first step is to turn the image to greyscale (*Image > Adjust > Greyscale*) (accept the default settings in the Filter Gallery) and then use the *Levels* dialog (*Image > Adjust > Levels*) to reduce the level of detail.

Moving the right and leftmost sliders towards the middle, and the middle slider slightly to the right, should produce a good result. We're aiming to create a strong contrast black and white image.

Original image

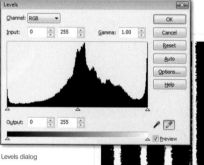

Levels dialog

Final result

STEP 2

We then create a new layer. Choosing a bright colour, in this case a strong pink, we use the *Paintbrush* tool to paint the area around the head a solid colour. Don't worry too much about being neat, just do the best you can.

Set the bend mode for the layer to *Lighten*.

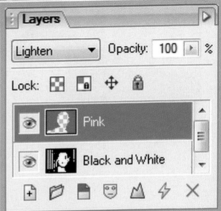

Layers tab

Pop Art

3

STEP 3

To add some colour to the lips, add a new layer, choose a bright red, and paint over the top of the lips. Now simply change the blend mode for that layer to *Screen*.

Layers tab

Final image

STEP 1 - Style 2

The first step is to trace the original, for this we use a separate layer. The standard *Paintbrush* tool is used and the main lines and detail picked out. To get that comic book look, try to draw your lines so that they taper towards either end.

Trace over original image

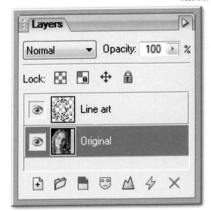

Layers tab

Pop Art

STEP 2

2

Then add extra layers and use the *Paintbrush* tool to fill in the areas of colour.

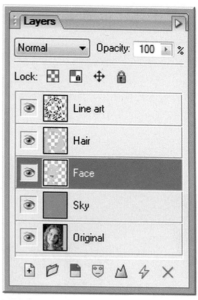

Layers tab

Line with colour

STEP 3

The only thing left to do is give the image that true 'comic book' feel. This is achieved by using the *Filter Gallery*.

Select one of your colour layers, choose the *Halftone Effect*, and then adjust the *Radius* value to achieve the desired effect.

Filter Gallery

Photo Prints

Turn your ordinary image into a realistic 3D print.

See how it was done...

Photo Prints

1

STEP 1 - PROJECT PREPARATION

Create a new image - 800 x 700, 96 dpi.
Make sure the background layer is filled with
white.

Choose an off-white foreground colour and
draw a rectangle in the centre of the
document. Name the layer 'photo background.'

Click *Layers > Effects > Effects...* and add a
drop shadow with the following settings:

> Opacity 30
> Blur 3
> Distance 0

2

STEP 2 - BRINGING IN AN IMAGE

Open an image to work with. Click *Select > Select All*. Then click *Edit > Copy*
and close the image. Click *Edit > Paste > As New Layer* to paste the image
into a new layer in your document (name your layer 'picture').

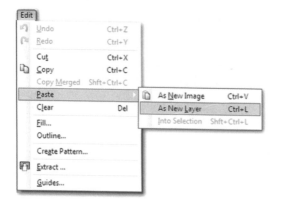

Photo Prints

STEP 3 - USING A MASK TO DISPLAY YOUR IMAGE IN THE PHOTO PRINT

Select your 'photo background' layer.

Click *Select > Create from Layer Alpha*.

Click *Select > Modify > Contract*, enter 5 pixels.

Add Layer Mask button

Select your 'picture' layer.

Mask icon

Click *Add Layer Mask* (the mask will now form outside of the selected area).

Un-link Mask icon

Click *Select > Deselect*.

On the *Layers* tab, click *Unlink Mask* and then use the *Move* tool to reposition the picture as required (but preserving the masks' position).

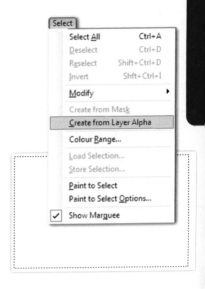

STEP 4 - ADD HIGHLIGHT EFFECTS TO THE PHOTO PRINT

Select your 'photo background' layer. Click *Select > Create from Layer Alpha*.

Create a new layer, name it 'highlights' and move the layer to the top.

Use the *Gradient Fill* tool with a 'black to 0% opaque' setting and draw in from the top left corner towards the centre (see next page).

Gradient sliders in the Gradient dialog

Gradient Fill tool

Do the same again, this time with a 'white to 0% opaque' setting progressing from the bottom right towards the centre.

Click *Select > Deselect Layer*, then change the layer's opacity to 50%

Photo Prints

Selected region and drawing the gradient from the top left corner

STEP 5 - ADD SHADOW TO PHOTO PRINT

Set the foreground colour to black.

Select the *Curved Outline* tool.

Draw a shape roughly like the one illustrated right.

Name the layer 'shadow' and move it below the 'photo print background' layer.

Node Edit tool

Select the *Node Edit* tool - you can use this to curve the straight lines, as illustrated.

Curved Outline tool

Right-click the layer on the *Layers* tab and choose *Rasterize*.

3 steps to getting your box shadow

Click *Effects > Blur > Gaussian Blur* and set the *Radius* to 6. Set the layer's opacity to 50%.

Position the shadow underneath the photo print until you've achieved the desired effect. The shadow should make the print look like it's lightly lifted off the background.

STEP 6 - FINISHING OFF

Ctrl-click all the layers in the *Layers* tab, except for the background layer.

Use the *Deform* tool to slightly rotate all layers – first click the *Unlink Mask* button to allow the image to rotate.

Deform tool

Duplicate the background layer and fill it with a different colour - experiment to find something that will make the photo print image stand out more. You could also use a background image to great effect with these photo prints - like a photo of a desk or a wall etc.

Your Layers tab should look similar to ours

Click the Mask icon on the right to select it on the picture layer

Moving and adjusting the image to fit inside the mask

Deform tool

STEP 7 - CHANGING THE IMAGE ON THE PHOTO PRINT

As we created a mask earlier to allow the image to show through, we can try out different images without repeating all the steps to make the photo print.

Duplicate the 'picture' layer, click the image thumbnail and press *Delete*.

You can then open another image, click *Select > Select All*. Then *Edit > Copy*. Close the image.

On the 'picture' layer, click *Select > Select All*, and then click *Edit > Paste > Into Selection*.

With the image thumbnail selected, click *Unlink Mask*.

Use the *Deform* tool to position the image as required.

Photo Prints

FINISHED - THAT'S IT!

Photo Art

Turn photos into art using filters and layer masks.

See how it was done...

TIP: You can create lots of creative material for your project using only one source photograph.. Just cut out interesting details.

Photos Into Art

In this project, we'll produce different 'art effects' from a sports car photograph, leading up to our final composition.

Using layers in PhotoPlus is a useful way of presenting various ideas and different versions of a finished composition. You'll see how the whole of this project can be achieved with one .spp PhotoPlus file.

Photos into Art

1 Black and White Background with a Colour Subject

To begin, we *duplicated* the layer so that we could refer back to the original image if necessary. We then *desaturated* the top layer.

Using a combination of hard and soft brushes, we selected the *Standard Eraser tool* and rubbed out the car from the desaturated layer (thus allowing the coloured layer to show through). Large soft brushes work for inner areas of the subject, whereas smaller soft and hard brushes are best for edge work.

The original colour layer can be duplicated again (which appears underneath the de-saturated layer) and a *Diffuse Glow* effect (*Effects* > *Render* > *Diffuse Glow*) applied to give the colour of the car a nice soft sheen.

The Standard Eraser tool is used on the desaturated layer - showing the coloured layer underneath

Layers tab

Standard Eraser tool

Brush Tip tab

Photos into Art

Black and White Drawing with a Colour Subject

In the same way as before, we duplicated the source layer to work on. This new top layer had the *Trace Contour* effect applied to it (*Effects > Edge> Find All*). It was then converted to *Greyscale* and *Brightness / Contrast* was tweaked. As before, the *Standard Eraser* tool was used on the subject in the layer to make the coloured layer show through.

Another variant on this effect is to create a *Selection* from the drawing layer , and then by inverting the selection you can isolate just a portion of the layer–any shape you require–and add a shadow and/or border to complete the effect....

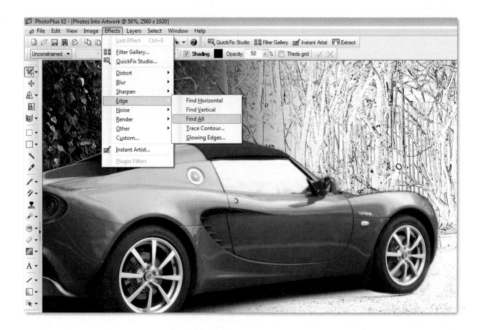

Background drawing effect

Isolated drawing effect

Photos into Art

3

Zoom Blur Background

This is a great effect that's easy to achieve. A duplicated layer of the photo has a *Zoom Blur* effect applied to it. Then the *Standard Eraser* tool (with a selection of hard and soft brushes) was used to rub out where the effect appears over the subject (the car) in the original layer.

You don't need to be too precise with the *Standard Eraser* tool for this effect, so it's really fun and quick to achieve!

Layers used for this effect

4

Stained Glass Background

Same as previous example, but substitute the *Zoom Blur* effect for *Effects > Other > Stained Glass*.

Layers tab

On the *Layers* tab, left, we can see all the different effects used throughout this project.

The top layer - the black & white drawing with its mask (which has a gradient applied) appears over the next visible layer (which acts as the source for the effect).

With a slight *Diffuse Glow* effect applied, the effect (shown on the following page) is completed > >

Layer Masked Background Drawing Effect

In a previous step, we already created a black and white background drawing effect on a layer. We'll now use it to achieve the above effect without permanently altering the layer. This can be done using layer masks.

With the 'drawing' layer selected, click *Layers > Mask > Add Mask > Reveal All*. This adds the layer mask, which by default will show the whole layer. The colour Black makes the layer transparent, whilst the colour White masks out the layer. So by selecting the layer mask and applying a gradient fill of Black through to White, we can produce an effect that blends the colourful background layer with the black and white drawing layer.

That's it! We've ended up with a composition that fades two different backgrounds underneath an enhanced subject at the forefront. Clever! See the facing page for a commercial example...

class leading performance and style

FAST CARS
MAGAZINE

Extraction

We'll look at various methods to cut out a subject from a photo and place it on another background.

See how it was done...

Extracting a Subject from a Photo

METHOD 1: Colour Selection Tool

The *Colour Selection* tool lets you select a consistently coloured area without the need to laboriously trace its outline. Options include the colour range, or tolerance, for the selection.

METHOD 2: Background Eraser Tool

The *Background Eraser* tool enables you to erase the background of an image, while maintaining an object (and its edges) in the foreground. It erases pixels on a layer to expose transparency as you drag your mouse over the area by specifying different sampling and tolerance options. It works by sampling a colour in the centre of the brush and deletes that colour wherever it appears within the brush area.

METHOD 3: Extraction Tool

Using the *Extraction* tool can be a more effective method to isolate a foreground object and remove it from its background. Intricate edges, wispy hair etc. , can be cut out with less manual work than other methods.

METHOD 4: Alpha Channels

This is a simple technique for masking the foreground object in an image using the *Channels* tab. Once an *Alpha Channel* is created, it can be loaded on the background layer and then the selection can be removed.

Extracting a Subject from a Photo

METHOD 1: Colour Selection Tool

The *Colour Selection* tool lets you select a consistently coloured area without the need to laboriously trace its outline. Options include the colour range, or *tolerance*, for the selection.

It's not the best method for removing the subjects in this image - as they are of a similar colour to the background.

Holding down the Shift key enables you to add to your selection

Colour Selection tool

Promote the background layer to a standard layer. Once your selection is deleted you will see a transparent background

Extracting a Subject from a Photo

METHOD 2: Background Eraser Tool

The *Background Eraser* tool enables you to erase the background while maintaining an object (and its edges) in the foreground. It erases pixels on a layer to expose transparency as you drag your mouse over the area by specifying different sampling and tolerance options. It works by sampling a colour in the centre of the brush and deletes that colour wherever it appears within the brush area.

Background Eraser tool

Using the Background eraser tool

This is a very effective technique for use on this image. The *Background Eraser* tool effectively finds the edges of the subject and proceeds to remove only the unwanted background. Only minor adjustments to the *tolerance* values and *brush sizes* were needed in order to get at the tricky parts.

Extracting a Subject from a Photo

METHOD 3: Extraction Tool

3

Using the *Extraction* tool can be a more effective method to isolate a foreground object and remove it from its background. Intricate edges, wispy hair etc. can be cut out with less manual work than other methods.

The *Edge Marker* tool paints an outline around the subject to be extracted. The subject is then filled using the *Foreground* tool.

 Edge Marker tool

 Foreground tool

The *Edge Marker* tool paints an outline around the subject to be extracted. The subject is then filled using the *Foreground Fill* tool.

Extraction dialog

Extracting a Subject from a Photo

Clicking *Preview* will display the extracted subject against a transparent background.

The extraction can be reverted in order to try again, or alternatively to make finer adjustments you can use the *Touchup* and *Edge Cleaner* tools on the subject while still in preview mode.

You can get great results with this method.

 Touchup tool

 Edge Cleaner tool

The resulting extract

Panoramic

We'll join up a series of photos to make a seamless panoramic shot.

See how it was done...

Panoramic Photos

STEP 1

Open your first photo in PhotoPlus. Promote the Background layer (right-click on the layer in the *Layers* tab, and click *Promote To Layer*), then set your canvas size (click *Image*, then *Canvas Size*) to something like *Width:* 300% and *Height:*120%. This will give you room to bring in the remaining photos you'll need for your panoramic composition.

Once you have your photos assembled, set all the layer blending modes to *Screen.* This will enable you to match up the photos. All the overlaps will be semi-transparent, allowing you to focus on subjects in the photos such as trees - lining them up so they match.

STEP 2

The photos will probably require further matching. You can create a selection area and then use the *Transform* or *Rotation* tools to shorten or lengthen section so that you can match them. You can now set all your layer blends back to *Normal*.

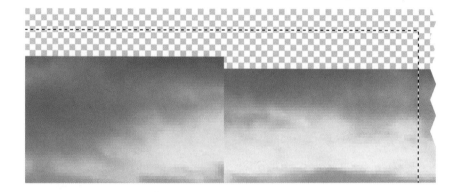

STEP 3

Your photos may also need some colour matching, achieved through use of the *Hue/Saturation/Lightness* and *Brightness/Contrast* dialogs.

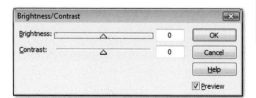

Panoramic Photos

STEP 4

When things are looking as close as can be at this stage, it's time to merge the layers.

Then we need to fix all the bits that still don't match up. We do this using the *Clone* tool. In the screenshots below note that a join line needs to be fixed. By cloning some of the cloud detail from the right, the join line is fixed.

You can see the merged layers don't match

Different brush sizes and setting were used

Clone tool

The image has been subtly cleaned up using clone brushes of varying sizes

STEP 5

The project canvas needs to be sized down to trim off all unwanted overlaps and edges. The *Crop* tool defines an area in your document which you wish to crop to. Once defined, double-click inside the crop area or click the *OK* button on the Context toolbar.

The flattened layer can now be edited as a whole and needs to be enhanced with use of the *Hue/Saturation/Lightness* dialog, the B*rightness/Contrast* dialog, and then additional filters as required.

We achieved a good effect by finishing off with a *Diffuse Glow* filter effect.

Panoramic Photos

That's it!

Take a look at some more finished panoramic compositions we've created using the very techniques discussed in this project...

Panoramic Photos

Whitby Coastline, UK. Panoramic Composition

Whitby Abbey, UK. Panoramic Composition

Daffodils in Nottingham, UK. Panoramic Composition

Glamorize

We took a normal portrait photo and quickly applied some useful techniques to glamorize it.

See how it was done...

Glamorizing a Portrait Photo

STEP 1

The source graphic required some 'touching up' work and a combination of the *Clone* tool and *Blur* tool is perfect for this.

Slightly blurring an area can subtly fade out wrinkles from a subject's skin.

 Blur tool

See how these closeups of original details have now been improved in the image to the right >

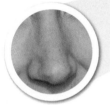

The *Clone* tool copies a portion of an image from a brush stroke - from a selected area (circled) to the destination area (crossed). Use varying brush tips to vary the area of cloning.

The image has been subtly cleaned up using cloning and blurring

Clone tool

Brush Tip tab

Brush Tip
Basic
• 16
• 32
• 64
• 128

Glamorizing a Portrait Photo

STEP 2

The *Diffuse Glow* filter is tremendously effective for changing the feel of an image.

We instantly get a glamorous sheen that serves to soften and brighten, while further smoothing out blemishes etc.

Layers tab

Black and white tends to reveal contrast and shadows in a photo – something that adds to making an image appear more glamorous.

We *desaturated* the image and tweaked the *brightness and contrast* settings slightly which brought us near to the end of our project.

Brightness/Contrast dialog

Glamorizing a Portrait Photo

3

STEP 3

The addition of a faded frame effect finishes this project nicely.

The screenshot below illustrates how it was quickly achieved - an *Inner Shadow* layer effect with a relatively high blur setting and a moderate opacity.

That's it!

Beach Scene Montage

STEP 4

Once all our composition layers had been prepared, it was time to fine-tune the overall appearance.

Colours were matched across each of the layers using the *Hue/Saturation/Lightness* and *Brightness/Contrast* dialogs.

Beach Scene Montage

The finished composition!

Vintage

This vintage photo was scanned and then enhanced in PhotoPlus.

See how it was done...

Vintage Photos

STEP 1

First the layer was *duplicated* – so that we could refer back to the original image if necessary. We then *desaturated* the image as the colour information wasn't needed in the edits.

There were several defects showing on the photo–some tearing, folding, and black spots. These were all corrected by using the *Clone* tool. Through brushwork, this replaces one area of the image with an identical copy (clone) from another part. – in this case, the brickwork in the photo. You can get good results by cloning a 'good' brick and then brushing over one that shows a defect.

Original scratches, rips, and spots

Image 'cleaned up'

STEP 2

What we saw immediately in the photo was a lack of detail in the children's faces. We zoomed into each face and then used the *Freehand Selection* tool to draw a rough selection around the features. This selection was then copied and pasted onto a new layer. With the layer blend set to *Burn*, our selection shows as a high contrasting enhancement. Next, we used the *Standard Eraser* tool (small brush size with *Hardness* set to 0) to erase the edges of the selection–taking care to only leave behind the enhanced features of eyes, mouth, and nose.

The selection layer at this point is still too high in contrast. We altered the *Opacity* of the layer until reaching a point where the details on the face were enhanced, but not to the detriment of contrast levels in the rest of the picture. This process was repeated for each child's face, and even in some other areas needing enhancement – for example, the fingers and hair.

Face details enhanced

Vintage Photos

STEP 3

The *Layers* tab shows the original image at the bottom, with the various stages of the project building up to the top layer.

Now it's time to *merge visible layers*. All separate opacity settings and layer blend modes are lost in this process as the composition is flattened. By doing so, however, the image is then easier to edit as a whole.

PhotoPlus layers for this project

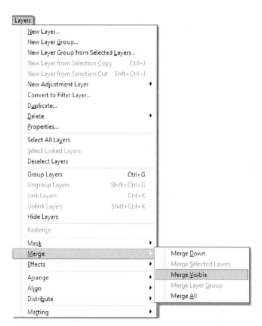

Merging the PhotoPlus layers

Nearly finished!

4

STEP 4

With all the layers merged, a *Diffuse Glow* effect is applied to the image. This softens and brightens the image, whilst still preserving much of the detail in the background and elsewhere..

That's it!

Vintage Photos

Here is another example, which used similar techniques to restore and enhance the original photo.

Grunge

This composition was created with multiple brushes and blended layers.

See how it was done...

Grunge Composition

STEP 1

This project will help you to create an abstract composition, the style of which would be suited to CD artwork or a movie poster. Random brushwork, imagery, layer blend effects and lots of imagination can create very emotive artwork.

Using a single colour, multiple brush work (from the *Effects - Earth* category) was applied over the same layer to build up a messy and interesting texture. Another layer was added, with similar brushwork.

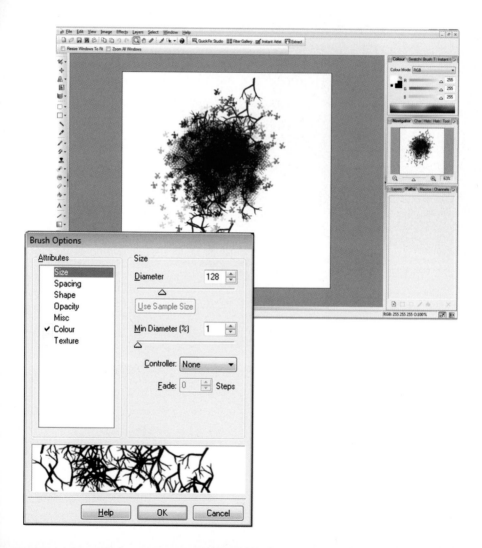

STEP 2

Adding a lower layer of random large brushwork (which was subsequently blurred using a strong *Gaussian Blur*) created further depth.

One of the top texture layers had its layer blend set to *Overlay* to offset some of the blue colouration.

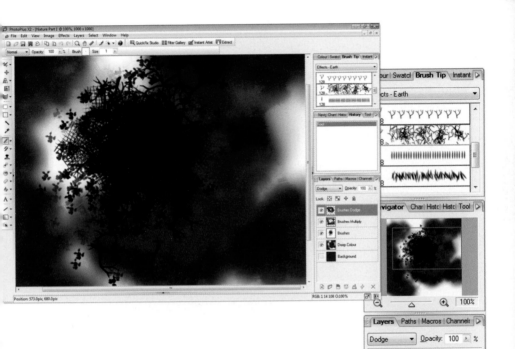

Grunge Composition

STEP 3

Another layer was created below the others, and was filled with dark blue. With the above layers now using various layer blending settings, the piece takes on a dark but multi-textured personality!

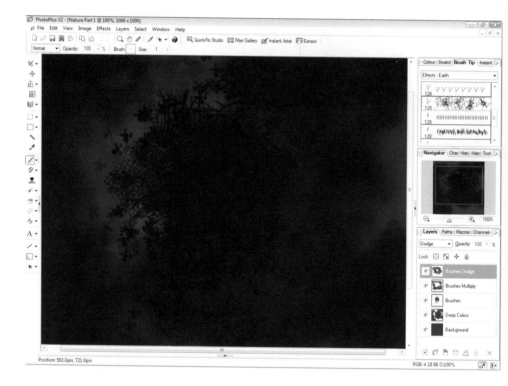

Grunge Composition

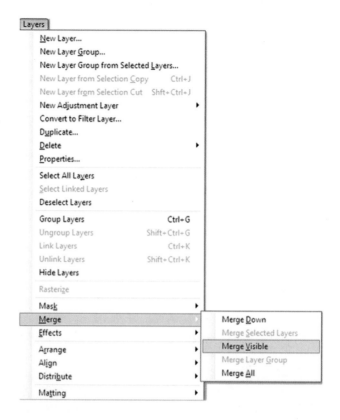

STEP 4

All of the layers were linked and merged.

This allows more freedom of editing to one complete layer–such as changing the colours easily, and applying project-wide effects. It's a very useful step in the process of creating multi-layered projects, but the downside is not being able to change any of the previous blending effects or erasing parts that made up the original layers.

It's like starting again from one layer. This can be solved by saving multiple versions of your project, so you can go back to particular stages.

Grunge Composition

STEP 5

Our single combined layer was then able to be manipulated as a whole. The *Hue/Saturation/Lightness*, and *Brightness/Contrast* settings were altered to bring out some of the dark details.

By duplicating this layer several times, with varying degrees of blur effects applied, and by using several layer blend mode settings (*Overlay, Dodge, Lightness,* etc*)* the scene can achieve a dramatic 'overexposed' bright new look.

With a few additional 'tweaks,' our composition has taken its finished shape.

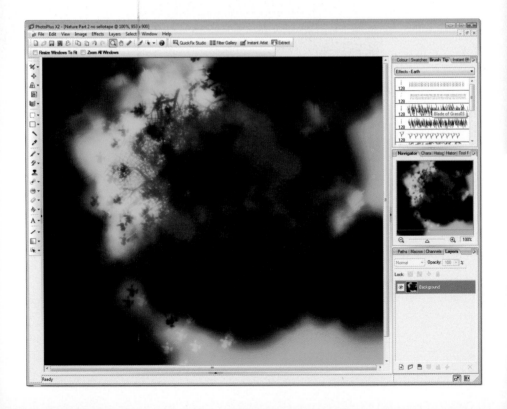

STEP 6

The addition of a few more textures–some scratches and a scanned image of some sticky tape strips complete our project. It could be beneficial to do further edits, with more brushwork and scratches to further decay and 'distress' the piece.

Grunge Composition

This shows an example of how an abstract composition such as the one created in this project can be used commercially.

Sketch

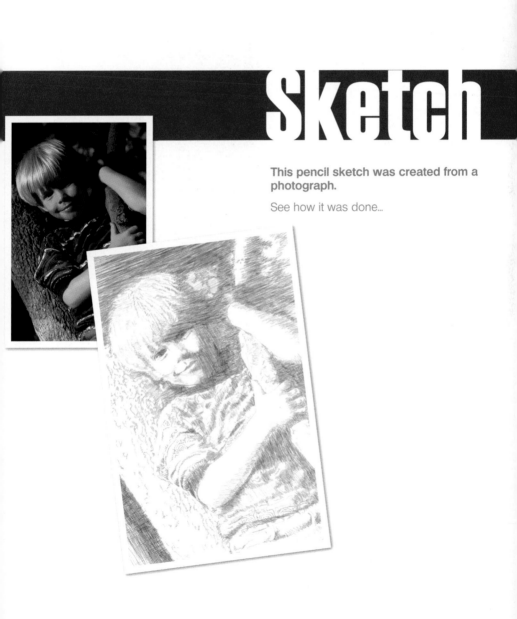

This pencil sketch was created from a photograph.

See how it was done...

Pencil Sketch

STEP 1

After choosing a nice image with good composition and decent lighting, we then chose a suitable brush tip, in this case a *Pencil* tip with a setting of just 5 pixels.

Original image

Paintbrush tool

Brush Tip

Media - Pencil

130

5

128

128

128

128

Brush Tip tab

Pencil Sketch

Opacity reduced

STEP 2

The image is desaturated using *Greyscale* (click *Image* then *Adjust*). We then reduce the *Opacity* of the layer and place a white layer underneath. This creates a trace image, with all pencil marks created on separate layers.

Layers tab

A new layer is created on which to draw the brush strokes. (A graphics tablet is an extremely useful tool to use for this sort of work instead of, or alongside, your mouse.)

We now start building up the tone with our small pencil brush. Simply pick out the areas of light and shadow and begin colouring. Remember that you don't have to be perfect and can always go back and correct any mistakes.

Pencil Sketch

3

STEP 3

By using a few separate layers you can easily divide your sketch up into areas of tonal value, working from light to dark and building up layer by layer. This makes it much simpler to rectify any mistakes, and lighten or darken the layer values.

Try to keep your strokes quick and simple, after all we are trying to produce a sketchy effect. Don't be afraid to experiment and make mistakes.

Layers tab

STEP 4

The final image... The process is complete
whenever you are happy with the results!

Pencil Sketch

This technique also lends itself to creating oil painting effects...

For this example, we chose *Paint Effect* brushes to build up our painting.

You can create truly unique artwork for use

In your documents - designs like these make great postcards or greetings cards!

Model World

Use this quick and easy technique to turn an everyday scene into a miniature model.

See how it was done...

Model World

STEP 1

Duplicate the Background layer:

- Open your image.

- On the **Layers** tab, right-click the Background layer and click **Duplicate**.

Original image

🔘 Using duplicate layers lets you apply your image adjustments experimentally. You can turn the layers on and off to compare 'before' and 'after' images. You can also easily edit or delete the corrections later.

STEP 2

Add a Gaussian Blur Filter Layer:

- Right-click the duplicate layer and click **Convert to Filter Layer**.

- In the **Filter Gallery**, click **Blur** and then click the **Gaussian** swatch. Set the **Radius** value to **5** and click **OK.**.

Gaussian blur applied

Model World

STEP 3

Add a Layer Mask:

- On the **Layers** tab, with the **Filter Layer** selected, click **Add Layer Mask**.
  - or -
  Or on the **Layers** menu, choose **Mask/Add Mask**, then **Reveal All**.

Add Layer Mask

STEP 4

Paint in the detail:

- On the **Colour** tab, set the foreground colour to black.

- With the mask selected, click the **Paintbrush** tool.

- On the **Brush Tip** tab or context toolbar, choose a large soft brush and then brush on the image to restore the detail.

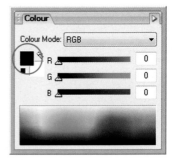

Paintbrush

💡 To get the best results, restore the detail in a horizontal band right across your image.

Model World

That's all there is to it!

If required, you can fine-tune your image by doing the following:

- Switch to a smaller brush size to work on more detailed areas.

- Change the foreground colour to grey to bring back partial focus to some areas.

- Adjust the Gaussian blur effect. To do this, simply double-click the Filter Layer to open the **Filter Gallery**, and then increase or reduce the **Radius** value.

Because we are used to looking down on models, this technique is most convincing when applied to photos taken from above (such as the example used in this project and the image pictured below right).

However, you can also achieve some interesting results with other images such as the one below left, which was taken at street level.

Scrapbook

Turn special memories into unique scrapbooks to treasure and keep.

See how it was done...

Making a Digital Scrapbook

STEP 1

Add your main background:

- In Windows Explorer, browse to the **Workspace\Scrapbook** folder. Drag **Background25.jpg** onto the PhotoPlus workspace.

- Switch to landscape orientation by clicking **Image/ Rotate/Image 90 Clockwise**.

- Save your file as **Page01.spp**.

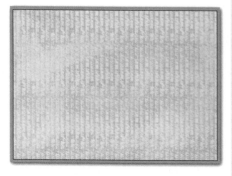

STEP 2

Add other background images:

- Drag **Background01.jpg** onto your workspace.

- On the **Layers** tab, you'll see that PhotoPlus adds this image as a new layer and selects it.

Creative resources

To complete your scrapbook, you'll need a range of backgrounds and creative elements. You can choose from the following options:

- Use our sample backgrounds and creative elements. In a standard installation, you'll find these in the following location: **C:\Program Files\Serif\PhotoPlus\X2\ Tutorials\Workspace\Scrapbook**

- Choose from the range of creative resources provided on the **PhotoPlus X2 Studio Extras DVD**.

- Create your own creative resources. For example, try scanning paper and fabric swatches, flowers, shells, leaves, and other objects that fit with your scrapbook theme. To learn how to extract scanned objects, such as leaves and flowers, from their backgrounds, see 'Replacing Backgrounds' (in the **Photography** tutorials section), or 'Extracting Subjects from Photos' (**Projects**).

This project assumes that you're using the **Workspace** folder samples.

Making a Digital Scrapbook

- Working on the **Background01** layer, use the **Move** tool to drag the image to the left, exposing **Background25** beneath it.

 Move tool

- Drag **Background09.jpg** from the Explorer window onto your page. Move it into position at the left edge of the page.

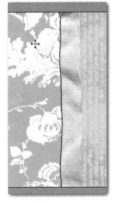

STEP 3

Add, resize, and rotate creative elements:

- Drag **Ribbon01.png** from the Explorer window onto your page. Move it into position as illustrated right.

- Drag **Tag.png** onto your page.
  With the **Tag** layer selected, click the **Deform** tool. A rectangular bounding box displays around the image.

 Deform tool

- To make the tag smaller, hold down the **Shift** key and then drag a corner handle inwards.

- To rotate the tag, drag from just outside a corner–you'll see the cursor change to the **Rotate** cursor.

Making a Digital Scrapbook

STEP 4

Add a drop shadow to the tag:

- At the bottom of the **Layers** tab, click the **Add Layer Effects** button.

- In the **Layer Effects** dialog, apply a **Drop Shadow** with the following settings:

 Add Layer Effects

  Opacity 77; **Blur** 10; **Distance** 2; **Angle** 45.

STEP 5

Add first photo:

- Drag **Photo_01.jpg** onto the page.

- Using the **Deform** tool, hold down the **Shift** key and drag a corner handle to resize the image.

 **Deform tool**

- Move the photo into position as illustrated left.

STEP 6

Add and recolour a frame:

- Drag **Large_White_Frame_L.png** onto the page. Resize it to fit on top of the photo.

- Click **Image/Adjust/Brightness & Contrast**. Set **Brightness** and **Contrast** to **100**.

- Repeat step 4 to apply a drop shadow to the frame.

Making a Digital Scrapbook

STEP 7

Merge and rotate photo and frame layers:

- On the **Layers** tab, hold down the **Ctrl** key and click to select both the **Large_White_Frame_L** and the **Photo_01** layers. Right-click the selected layers and then click **Merge Selected Layers**.

- Right-click the new merged layer and click **Properties**. Rename the layer **Photo1**.

- Use the **Deform** tool to rotate and position the photo and frame.

STEP 8

Add twirl and flower elements and adjust colour and opacity:

- Drag **Twirl02.png** and **Flower_Stem.png** onto the page.

- On the **Twirl02** layer, click **Image/Adjust** then **Hue/Saturation/Lightness**. Set **Lightness** to 100. On the **Layers** tab, reduce the layer **Opacity** to 50%.

- Working on the **Flower_Stem** layer, click **Image/Adjust** then **Hue/Saturation/Lightness**. Set **Lightness** to 100. Repeat step 4 to apply a drop shadow to the flower.

- Use the **Deform** and **Move** tools to resize and position these two elements.

Move tool

Making a Digital Scrapbook

STEP 9

Add titles and captions:

- Click the **Text** tool and then click on your page to set the text insertion point.

- On the context toolbar, choose a font style and size. Click the square colour swatch. In the **Adjust Colour** dialog, set your font colour. For our title, we used 72 pt Times New Roman Italic in RGB (165, 136, 81).

- Type your text.

- Use the **Deform** tool to rotate and resize the text object.

- Repeat for each required text object.

STEP 10

Add final images and creative elements:

- Add **Photo_02.jpg** and **Photo_03.jpg** to the page and frame them.

- Add the **Brooch.png** and **Heart.png** elements and apply drop shadows. To change the colour of the heart, select the **Heart** layer and click **Image/Adjust** then **Hue/Saturation/Lightness**. Set the following values: **Hue** 51; **Saturation** 52; **Lightness** 8.

Congratulations, your first scrapbook page is complete!

💡 You can use the same backgrounds and creative elements to create a variety of page layouts. See our **Page01.Spp** and **Page02.Spp** samples in the **Workspace\Scrapbook** folder.

Makeover Studio

3

Introduction

In this chapter, we focus our attention on digital makeover techniques. Whether you want to remove under-eye dark circles, whiten teeth, smooth out skin, or erase a blemish, these retouching tricks will enhance any portrait photo. (Whether or not you choose to let your subject in on the secret is up to you!)

Index

Removing red eye

Use the **Red Eye** tool to correct the red eye effect often seen in colour photos taken with a flash. You can apply this correction on a duplicate layer (recommended), or directly to your image.

before

> 🔘 Using duplicate layers lets you apply the changes experimentally, without changing your original image. You can turn the layers on and off to compare 'before' and 'after' images. You can also easily edit or delete the corrections later.
>
> We suggest you choose meaningful names for your layers, for example, Red Eye Correction, Whiten Teeth, and so on.

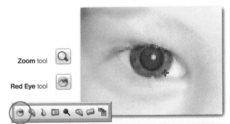

1 On the **Layers** tab, right-click the layer containing your image and then click **Duplicate**. In the **Duplicate Layer** dialog, name your layer and click **OK**.

2 On the Standard toolbar, click the **Zoom** tool and then click to zoom in on the subject's pupil.

3 On the Retouch Tools flyout, click the **Red Eye** tool.

Zoom tool

Red Eye tool

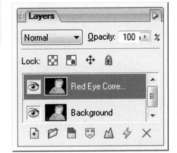

4 Move the cursor over the area to be fixed and click once.

- or -

Click and drag to draw an ellipse around the red area and then release the mouse button. (Don't make the ellipse too large as you may affect other red-based areas of the photo.

after

Whitening teeth and eyes

Whitening teeth and eyes

Use the **Dodge** tool to quickly whiten a smile and brighten eyes. Again, we'll apply this correction on a duplicate layer.

1 On the **Layers** tab, right-click the layer containing your image and then click **Duplicate**. In the **Duplicate Layer** dialog, name your layer and click **OK**.

2 On the **Layers** tab, select the duplicate layer and set the layer **Opacity** to **50%**.

3 On the Standard toolbar, click the **Zoom** tool and then click on your image to zoom into the mouth or eye area.

4 On the Retouch Tools flyout, click the **Dodge** tool.

5 On the context toolbar, in the **Tones** drop-down list, select **Midtones**.

6 On the **Brush Tip** tab, in the **Basic** category,, you'll find a range of soft and hard brushes, listed in that order, in sizes from 1 to 256 pixels. Select a small soft brush tip.

7 Click and drag over the teeth, or the whites of the eyes, to brighten them.

before

after

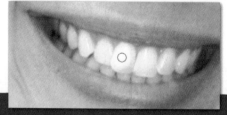

> ❗ To reduce or increase the whitening effect, adjust the layer o**pacity**.

Zoom tool 🔍

Dodge tool 🔍

Removing blemishes

PhotoPlus provides several tools for removing skin blemishes and flaws. All of the following techniques can be applied directly to an image, but for best practice, we'll use duplicate layers for methods 1 and 2 and a transparent layer for method 3.

Method 1: Blemish Remover

Use the **Blemish Remover** to remove small skin blemishes and other flaws.

1 On the **Layers** tab, right-click the layer containing your image and then click **Duplicate**. In the **Duplicate Layer** dialog, name your layer and click **OK**.

> To rename a layer after you have created it, right-click the layer and click **Properties**.

before

2 On the Tools toolbar, on the Repair Tools flyout, select the **Blemish Remover**.

after

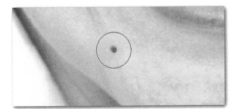

3 On the context toolbar, set your **Blemish Remover** tip size–this will depend on the region under repair.

4 Click on the blemish to define the target area.

Blemish Remover

5 Drag to select a suitable pickup area to replace the blemish (the outlined target area updates as you drag), then release the mouse button to apply the correction.

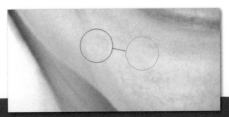

Removing blemishes

Method 2: Patch tool

Use the **Patch** tool to remove irregular shaped blemishes and flaws.

1 On the **Layers** tab, right-click the layer containing your image and then click **Duplicate**. In the **Duplicate Layer** dialog, name your layer and click **OK**.

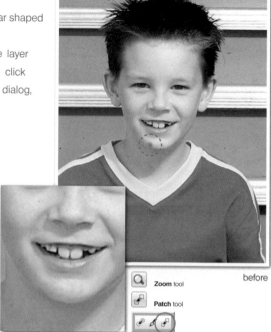

before

after

2 On the Standard toolbar, click the **Zoom** tool and then click on your image to zoom into the area you want to work on.

Zoom tool

Patch tool

3 On the Tools toolbar, on the Repair Tools flyout, select the **Patch** tool.

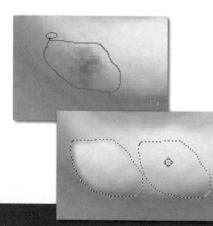

4 Click and drag on your image to outline the area you want to remove.

5 Drag the selected area over to a suitable pickup area to replace the blemish. The outlined target area updates as you drag.

6 Release the mouse button to apply the correction. Repeat as required.

7 To adjust the effect, drag the **Opacity** slider on the **Layers** tab.

Removing blemishes

Method 3: Clone tool

Use the **Clone** tool to cover flaws, or remove unwanted areas, by copying a selection from one area to another.

1   On the **Layers** tab, click [+] **New Layer**. In the **Layer Properties** dialog, name your layer and click **OK**. PhotoPlus adds a new transparent layer to the **Layers** tab.

before

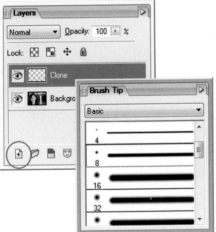

 Clone tool

2   On the Tools toolbar, on the Clone Tools flyout, click the **Clone** tool.

3   On the **Brush Tip** tab, or context toolbar, choose a brush tip (generally soft-tipped is best, but this will depend on your image).

4   On the context toolbar, set your brush tip size–this will depend on the region under repair, and select the **Use all layers** check box.

5   Press and hold down the **Shift** key and then click to define a pickup point.

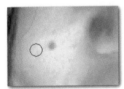

6   Hold down the mouse button and brush on the image to lay down paint (the cross-hair indicates the region being copied). Release the mouse button to end the stroke.

after

Removing dark circles

There are several techniques you can use to remove under-eye dark circles.

- **Paintbrush:** Use this method for a smooth, airbrushed effect.

- **Curves adjustment:** Use this method when more subtle results are required.

- **Patch tool:** Use this method to replace dark circles with a selected lighter area.

Method 1: Paintbrush

Use the **Paintbrush** to paint out dark circles. We'll use a duplicate layer for this technique.

1 On the **Layers** tab, right-click the layer containing your image and then click **Duplicate.** In the **Duplicate Layer** dialog, name your layer and click **OK.**

2 On the Standard toolbar, click the **Zoom** tool and then click on your image to zoom into the eye area.

3 On the Tools toolbar, click the **Colour Pickup** tool.

4 On the context toolbar, in the drop-down list, select **3 x 3 Average.**

5 Click on a suitable area of the skin to use as a colour to paint over the dark circles.
   Over on the **Colour** tab, the **Foreground** colour swatch updates with the new pickup colour.

before

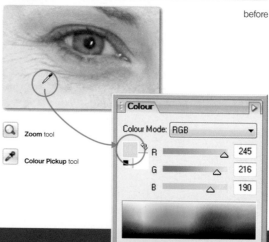

Zoom tool

Colour Pickup tool

Removing dark circles

7 On the Tools toolbar, click the **Paintbrush**.

8 On the context toolbar, set the blend mode to **Lightness** and the **Opacity** to 20%.

9 On the **Brush Tip** tab or context toolbar, select a small soft brush tip and then brush over the dark circles to lighten them.

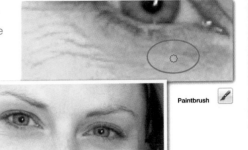

Paintbrush

after

Method 2: Curves adjustment

Use a **Curves adjustment** to minimize dark circles by adjusting tonal balance. We'll use an adjustment layer and a layer mask for this photo correction.

1 On the **Layers** tab, click 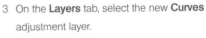 **New Adjustment Layer** and then click **Curves**.

2 In the **Curves** dialog, drag the centre of the diagonal line up, to form a gentle curve. (As you do this, you'll see your image lighten slightly.) Click **OK**.
   PhotoPlus adds a new **Curves** adjustment layer to the **Layers** tab.

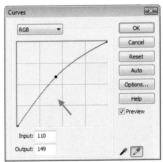

3 On the **Layers** tab, select the new **Curves** adjustment layer.

4 On the **Layers** menu, select **Mask/Add Mask/Hide All**. (Your image darkens as the **Curves** adjustment is hidden by the mask.)

5 On the **Layers** tab, PhotoPlus adds a mask to the **Curves** adjustment layer.

Removing dark circles

6 On the **Layers** tab, on the **Curves** adjustment layer, select the mask.

7 On the Tools toolbar, click the **Paintbrush**, then on the context toolbar, set the tool's blend mode to **Normal** and the **Opacity** to 100%.

8 On the **Colour** tab, set the foreground colour to white.

9 On the **Brush Tip** tab or context toolbar, select a small soft brush tip and then brush over the dark circles.

10 To adjust the effect, on the **Layers** tab, drag the layer **Opacity** slider.

Paintbrush

before

after

Removing dark circles

Method 3: Patch tool

Use the new **Patch** tool to replace dark circles with a lighter area of skin. We will make this correction on a duplicate layer.

1 On the **Layers** tab, right-click the layer containing your image and then click **Duplicate**. In the **Duplicate Layer** dialog, name your layer and click **OK**.

2 On the Standard toolbar, click the **Zoom** tool and then click on your image to zoom into the eye area.

3 On the Tools toolbar, on the Repair Tools flyout, click the **Patch** tool.

4 Click and drag on your image to outline the area you want to remove.

5 Drag the selected area over to a suitable pickup area to replace the blemish.

6 Release the mouse button to apply the correction.

7 To adjust the effect, on the **Layers** tab, drag the layer **Opacity** slider.

before

after

Smoothing skin

You can use any of the following techniques to create smoother, softer looking skin. The technique you choose depends on your subject matter and the overall effect you want to achieve.

Method 1: Gaussian Blur and Paintbrush 1

Blurs and softens facial lines and other flaws without affecting the rest of the image. This technique can produce subtle or dramatic results.

before

1 On the **Layers** tab, right-click the layer containing your image and then click **Duplicate**. In the **Duplicate Layer** dialog, click **OK**.

2 Right-click the duplicate layer and then click **Convert to Filter Layer**.

3 In the **Filter Gallery**, expand the **Blur** category and click the **Gaussian** swatch. Set the **Radius** to 20 and click **OK**.

PhotoPlus applies the blur effect and adds a new **Filter Layer** to the **Layers** tab.

Smoothing skin

4 On the **Layers** tab, select the filter layer. On the **Layers** menu, select **Mask/Add Mask/Hide All**.

5 On the **Layers** tab, select the mask and set the layer **Opacity** to **50%.**

6 On the Standard toolbar, click the **Zoom** tool and click on your image to zoom into the area to be smoothed.

7 On the Tools toolbar, click the **Paintbrush**.

8 On the **Colour** tab, set the **Foreground** colour swatch to white.

9 Select a small soft brush tip, and then brush over the skin to smooth it.

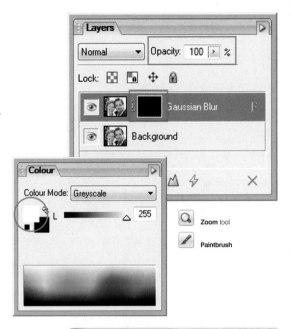

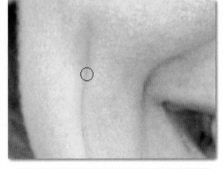

after

> 💧 **To increase or decrease smoothing:**
> On the **Layers** tab, adjust the layer opacity.
> - or -
> Double-click the **Filter Layer** and then adjust the **Radius** setting of the Gaussian blur effect.

Zoom tool

Paintbrush

Smoothing skin

Method 2: Scratch Remover

Blends and softens discrete areas of the image only–laughter lines, frown lines, and so on–without affecting the rest of the image. This technique is great when you want subtle results.

1 On the **Layers** tab, right-click the layer containing your image and then click **Duplicate**. In the **Duplicate Layer** dialog, name your layer and click **OK**.

2 On the **Layers** tab, select the duplicate layer and set the layer **Opacity** to **50%**.

before

after

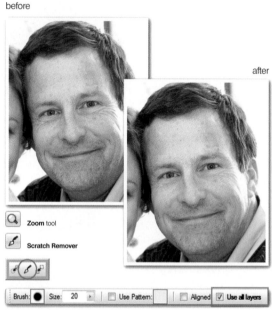

3 On the Standard toolbar, click the **Zoom** tool. Click on your image to zoom into the area to be smoothed.

4 On the Repair Tools flyout, click the **Scratch Remover**.

5 On the context toolbar, select **Use all layers**.

6 On the **Brush Tip** tab, or context toolbar, choose a small soft brush tip.

7 Press and hold down the **Shift** key and then click to define a pickup point.

8 Brush on the area you want to smooth. When you stop brushing, the surrounding colour flows into the repaired region.

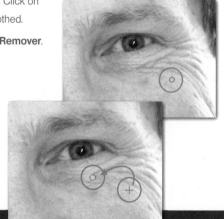

Smoothing skin

Method 3: Gaussian Blur and Paintbrush 2

Gives all areas of skin a smooth silky feel, while keeping facial details (eyes, lips, teeth, and so on) sharp. This technique is particularly suited to portrait and glamour shots.

1 On the **Layers** tab, right-click the layer containing your image and click **Duplicate**. In the **Duplicate Layer** dialog, type **Blur** and click **OK**.

2 Right-click the duplicate layer and then click **Convert to Filter Layer**.

3 In the **Filter Gallery**, expand

before   after

the **Blur** category and click the **Gaussian Blur** swatch. Set the **Radius** to **5** and click **OK**.

4 On the **Layers** tab, select the filter layer. On the **Layers** menu, select **Mask/Add Mask/Reveal All**.

5 On the **Layers** tab, select the mask and set the layer **Opacity** to **50%**.

6 On the Standard toolbar, click the **Zoom** tool. Click on your image to zoom into the area where you want to restore detail.

Smoothing skin

7 On the Tools toolbar, click the **Paintbrush**.

8 On the **Colour** tab, set the **Foreground** colour swatch to black.

9 Select a small soft brush tip, and then paint over the facial details you want to sharpen.

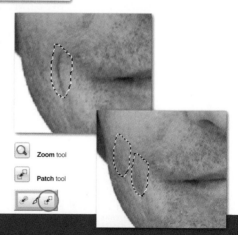

Method 4: Patch tool

This method replaces wrinkles with a selected area of smoother skin.

before   after

1 On the **Layers** tab, right-click the layer containing your image and then click **Duplicate**. In the **Duplicate Layer** dialog, name your layer and click **OK**.

2 Click the **Zoom** tool, and then click on the area to be worked on.

3 On the Repair Tools flyout, click the **Patch** tool.

4 Click and drag on your image to outline the area you want to smooth.

5 Drag the selected area over to a suitable pickup area to replace the blemish (the outlined target area updates as you drag), then release the mouse button to apply the correction.

6 To increase or reduce the effect, adjust the layer opacity.

Adding sparkle to eyes

Use this simple technique to bring your portrait photos to life. We'll show you how to apply an **Unsharp Mask** and a mask, and then use the **Paintbrush** to sharpen the eye area.

before   after

1   On the **Layers** tab, right-click the layer containing your image and then click **Duplicate**. In the **Duplicate Layer** dialog, name your layer and click **OK**. On the **Layers** tab, right-click the duplicate layer and click **Convert to Filter Layer**.

2   In the **Filter Gallery**, expand the **Sharpen** category and click the thumbnail swatch. Set the **Amount** to **150**, **Radius** and **Threshold** to **2**, and click **OK**.

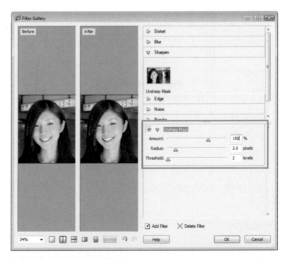

Adding sparkle to eyes

3 On the **Layers** tab, select the filter layer. On the **Layers** menu, select **Mask/Add Mask/Hide All**.

4 On the **Layers** tab, select the mask and set the layer **Opacity** to **75%**.

5 On the Standard toolbar, click the **Zoom** tool and click on your image to zoom into the eye area.

6 On the Tools toolbar, click the **Paintbrush**.

Zoom tool

Paintbrush

7 On the **Colour** tab, set the foreground colour to white.

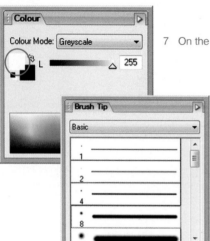

8 On the **Brush Tip** tab or context toolbar, select a small soft brush tip.

9 Paint over the eyes to sharpen.

10 To adjust the effect, on the **Layers** tab, adjust the layer opacity.

- or -

Double-click the filter layer and then adjust the **Unsharp Mask** settings.

For the ultimate in eye enhancement, combine this technique with the whitening method described previously (p. 256).

Removing hotspots

Use the **Clone** tool to remove or reduce hotspots and glare caused by uneven lighting or your camera's flash. We'll use a duplicate layer for this photo correction.

before   after

1 On the **Layers** tab, right-click the layer containing the image you want to work on and click **Duplicate**. In the **Duplicate Layer** dialog, name your layer and click **OK**.

2 On the **Layers** tab, select the duplicate layer.

3 On the Tools toolbar, click the **Clone** tool.

Clone tool

4 On the context toolbar, set the blend mode to **Darken**; set the **Opacity** to **50%**; and select the **Use all layers** check box.

5 On the context toolbar or **Brush Tip** tab, select a large soft brush tip.

6 Hold down the **Shift** key and then click once in an area of skin with no hotspots.

7 Brush over the hotspots to fade them.

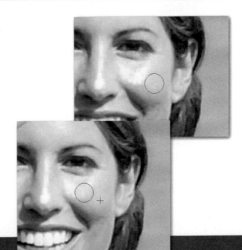

Faking a suntan

Faking a suntan

We'll use a transparent layer for this quick and easy photo enhancement.

1 On the **Layers** tab, click  **New Layer**. In the **Layer Properties** dialog, name your layer and click **OK**. PhotoPlus adds a new transparent layer to the **Layers** tab.

2 On the **Layers** tab, select the new layer. Set the blend mode to **Soft Light** and the **Opacity** to **50%**.

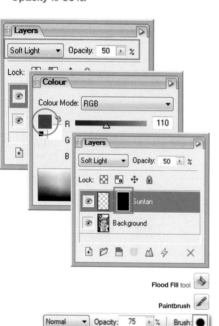

Flood Fill tool

Paintbrush

3 On the Tools toolbar, click the **Flood Fill** tool.

4 On the **Colour** tab, set the foreground colour to brown (we used RGB 110, 80, 41).

5 Click on the image to apply a brown fill to the layer.

6 On the **Layers** menu, select **Mask/Add Mask/Hide All**.

7 On the **Layers** tab, select the mask.

8 Click the **Zoom** tool and click on the image to zoom into the area to be worked on first.

9 Click the **Paintbrush**. On the context toolbar, set the blend mode to **Normal** and the **Opacity** to **75%**.

10 On the **Colour** tab, set the foreground colour to white.

11 Select a soft brush tip, and then paint over the skin.

12 Adjust the layer opacity to reduce or increase the depth of the suntan.

Slimming down

Use the **Deform** tool to quickly trim a few pounds from your subject!

before

after

1 On the Tools toolbar, click the **Deform** tool.

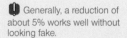 **Deform** tool

2 A rectangular bounding box, with sizing handles displays around the image.

3 Drag one of the side handles horizontally towards the centre of the image.

4 The further you drag, the slimmer the subject becomes.

> ⚠ Generally, a reduction of about 5% works well without looking fake.

Macros

4

Introduction

Macros

A macro is a saved sequence of steps (for example, commands, keyboard strokes, or mouse clicks) that can be stored and then recalled at a later date with a single command or keyboard stroke. Macros are particularly useful for storing multi-step tasks that are carried out repeatedly, or complex procedures that are time-consuming to reproduce.

In addition to allowing you to create your own macros (see the "Macros and Batch Processing" tutorial), PhotoPlus provides you with an extensive selection of predefined macros. With these, you can quickly and easily enhance, manipulate, and apply creative effects to your images.

On the **Macros** tab, in the drop-down list, the following predefined macro categories are available for selection:

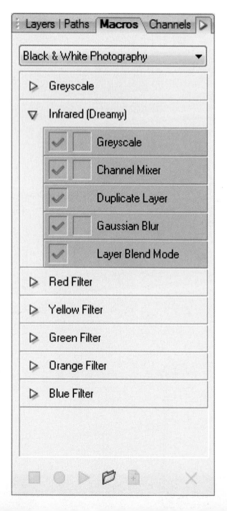

- •Black & White Photography
- •Colour
- •Commands
- •Effects
- •Frames
- •Gradient Maps
- •Layout Blurs
- •New Document Landscape (print)*
- •New Document Landscape (screen)*
- •New Document Portrait (print)*
- •New Document Portrait (screen)*
- •Photography
- •Selection
- •Text Effects
- •Text Outlines
- •Textures
- •Vignettes

These macros are not documented in this Resource Guide.

To see the various steps associated with a macro, click the arrow to the left of the macro name. The check boxes allow you to disable and enable each step. Some macros— for example, Effects/Pen Sketch—let you choose to open a relevant dialog to allow customization of the macro settings.

For more information on macro settings, see the *PhotoPlus User Guide* or online Help.

Black & White Photography

The **Black & White Photography** macros allow you to apply filter effects and techniques used in this style of photography.

You could apply the **Infrared (Dreamy)** option to make your image look like a fine art print, or you could apply the **Greyscale** option to make an image have a documentary feel, similar to the style of images used in newspapers.

Original

Infrared (Dreamy)

Greyscale

Colour Filters

Colour filters in the **Black & White Photography** category allow you to make an image black and white while also correcting or emphasizing any of the colours in the original image.

Red Filter **Yellow Filter** **Green Filter** **Orange Filter** **Blue Filter**

Apply a
Red Filter

Apply a
Yellow Filter

Apply a
Green Filter

Apply a
Orange Filter

Apply a
Blue Filter

Colour

The **Colour** macros allow you to apply a 'colour wash' effect to an image. For example, you might want to create a particular mood—try the **Recolour Blue** option; instantly "age" your photo-**Recolour Sepia**; or simply recolour an image to fit in with a particular colour scheme.

Original

Greyscale

Convert to greyscale image

Recolour Red

Image coloured red using Hue/Saturation/ Lightness

Recolour Blue

Image coloured blue

Recolour Green

Image coloured green

Recolour Orange

Image coloured orange

Recolour Yellow

Image coloured yellow

Recolour Sepia

Add a 'sepia' tone

Recolour Pink

Image coloured pink

Recolour Purple

Image coloured purple

Recolour (options)

Settings used
Hue -150
Saturation 50
Lightness 0

Recolour image with a colour of your choice

Quad Colour

Different coloured quadrants in image

Colour Stripes

Image coloured with different coloured stripes

Commands

The **Commands** macros provide you with a selection of commonly-used commands, such as **Copy**, **Paste**, **Rotate**, and **Crop**. Use these macros to facilitate the basic functionality of PhotoPlus. For example, run the **Canvas Size** macro to adjust your canvas dimensions; use **Flip Horizontal** to create a mirror image.

Original
with selection area illustrated
by ⌐⌐

Cut (selection)

Selection cut from image

Paste (new layer)

Selection pasted as new layer

Copy (selection)

Selection area copied

Crop (selection)

Image cropped to size of selection

Revert

Revert back to original image

Canvas Size

Canvas cropped to specific size
(250 x 350 pixels)

Image Size

Canvas resized to specific size
(250 x 350 pixels)

Flip Horizontal (layer)

Layer flipped horizontally

Flip Vertical (layer)

Layer flipped vertically

Rotate 90 CW

Layer rotated 90° clockwise

Rotate 90 ACW

Layer rotated 90° anti-clockwise

Rotate 180

Layer rotated 180°

Flatten Image

All layers in image flattened to give a single layer

Fill

Settings used
Colour R 219 G 35 B 193
Mode Screen
Opacity 50%

Fill selection with colour

Clear

Clear

Effects

Use the **Effects** macros to quickly apply your favourite creative effects to your images. PhotoPlus provides a range of effects, which you can use to produce subtle or dramatic results. Add a 'retro' feel to a portrait with **40's Glamour Model**. Soften and blur an image with **Dream**. For more extreme effects, try **Art** or **Shaken**.

Original
with selection area illustrated
by ⌞⌝, where applicable

Pencil Sketch

Image converted into
a pencil sketch

Pen Sketch

Image converted into
a pen sketch

Art

Image reproduced as
Pop Art

Heavy Pencil Sketch

Image converted into
a heavy pencil sketch

Soft Pastel

Image converted into
a soft pastel sketch

40's Glamour Model

Black and white soft
focus effect applied to
image

60's Sci-Fi

New Hue and
Saturation values
applied to image

Negative

Image converted into
a negative

Vintage Photo

Sepia colour wash and
soft focus applied to
image

Wobble

Wave distortion effect
applied to image

Shaken

A fragment blur is
applied to the image

Dream

A diffuse glow is
applied to the image

Effects

Disco

Neon effect applied to image edges

Quick Sketch

Image converted into a quick sketch

Girl Pop

Filter effect applied to image

Section Blur

Blurred effect applied to selected area of image

Night Vision

Lens distortion effect applied to the image

Multi Flares

Multi-coloured lens flares applied to image

Amoeba

Image is abstracted

Frames/Gradient Maps

Frames

The **Frames** macros allow you to frame your images with a single click. Frame styles range from basic to classic and modern, all including a matte surround.

Original

Basic

Basic with options

Matte Surround

Matte surround with options

Frame and Surround

Frame and surround with options

Wood Frame

Wood Frame and Surround

Modern Frame

Modern Frame and Surround

Metal Frame

Metal Frame and Surround

Gradient Maps

You can use the **Gradient Fill** tool, and the **Gradient** dialog settings to apply a predefined colour scheme to an image. You can also use the **Gradient Maps** macros to produce your favourite effects with a single command. Turn your colour photos into dramatic black and white images with the **Black and White** macro, or give an image an instant art effect with **Pop Art**.

Original

Gradient Maps

Black and White

Colours in the image are mapped to the basic Black to White Gradient Map

Red

Colours in the image are mapped to a Red to White Gradient Map

Pop Art

Colours in the image are mapped to a Blue to Yellow to Red Gradient Map

Summer

Colours in the image are mapped to a Red to Yellow to White Gradient Map

Black and White Mood

The image appears overexposed

Hot Pink

Colours in the image are mapped to a Red to Pink Gradient Map

Green

Colours in the image are mapped to a Green to White Gradient Map

Blue

Colours in the image are mapped to a Blue to White Gradient Map

Yellow

Colours in the image are mapped to a Yellow to Gradient Map

Orange

Colours in the image are mapped to an Orange to White Gradient Map

Purple

Colours in the image are mapped to a Purple to White Gradient Map

Pink

Colours in the image are mapped to a Pink to White Gradient Map

Rainbow

Colours in the image are mapped to a multi-coloured Gradient Map

Layout Blurs

Use the **Layout Blurs** macros to apply a range of blur effects to your images. For example, you can blur the edges of an image, while keeping the centre in focus; blur just the upper or lower portions of an image; or even 'frame' a photo with a larger, blurred version of the same image.

Original

Centred Image

Centred Small Image
Big Blur

Centred Image

Centred Small Image
Big B+W Blur

Centred Image

Centred Image Blur
Surround

Centred Image

Centred Image B+W
Blur Surround

Section Blur

Right Section Blur

Section Blur

Left Section Blur

Section Blur

Top Section Blur

Section Blur

Bottom Section Blur

Photography

Photography

Use the **Photography** macros to apply a range of photographic effects to your images. For example, you can change the exposure settings, sharpen an image, reduce saturation, or adjust brightness and contrast settings.

Original

Overexposed	**Underexposed**	**Sharpen Image**	**Reduce Saturation**	**Quick Brightness & Contrast**

Change exposure settings	Change exposure settings	Change focus settings	Reduce light saturation	Adjust brightness and contrast

Remove Dust + Scratches

Provides a quick fix for dusty or scratched photos, in the example below, we have restored a damaged image with the help of this macro!

Before   After

Selection Macros

Grow Selection
Expands a selected area of an image to include all adjacent areas with the same colour value.

Find Similar
Identifies and selects all areas of an image that have the same colour value as the selected area.

Contract by 1 pixel
Reduces the size of a selected area by one pixel around its border.

Expand by 1 pixel
Increases the size of a selected area by one pixel around its border.

Border
Creates a second selection around the original selected area, forming a 'selection border.'

Feather
Crops a selected area and softens its border.

Feather and Centre
Crops a selected area, centres it, and softens its border.

Centre
Crops a selected area and centres it.

Centre – Shadow
Crops a selected area, centres it, and adds a shadow around its border.

Text Effects

Use the **Text Effects** macros to apply a range of creative effects of the text in your images.

X2

Original

Spray Paint

Underwater

Water's Edge

Fuzz

Metal

Cut Out

Text Outlines

Use the **Text Outlines** macros to apply a range of outline effects to your text.

Simple White	Rainbow	Gradient White
X2	X2	X2

Simple White	Rainbow	Gradient White
X2	X2	X2

Simple White	Rainbow	Gradient White
X2	X2	X2

Simple White	Rainbow
	X2

Textures

The **Textures** macros allow you to add a variety of 'effects' to your images. You can apply a simple **Wood** or **Stone** texture, or see your photos "reproduced" on **Canvas** or **Recycled Paper**. Enable the dialogs and experiment with the various settings to produce some interesting results.

Textures

Original

Wood

Ripple

Canvas

Corrugated

Recycled Paper

Stone

Carved

Candy

Lava

Crumble

Skin

Water

Textures

Vignettes

Vignettes

Use the **Vignettes** macros to apply a range of surrounds. For example, apply a simple softened surround with **Oval Blur**; add and adjust filter effects by choosing **Oval Blur w/options**.

Original

Oval Blur

Oval Large Blur

Oval Blur w/options

Customize your own **Oval Blur** effect in the **Filter Gallery** dialog. In this instance, we applied a **Glass** effect from the **Distort** category of the **Filter Gallery**.

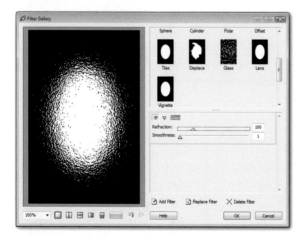

Vignettes

Square Blur

Square Large Blur

Square Blur w/options

Customize your own **Square Blur** effect in the **Filter Gallery** dialog. In this instance, we applied a **Fragment** effect from the **Blur** category of the **Filter Gallery**.

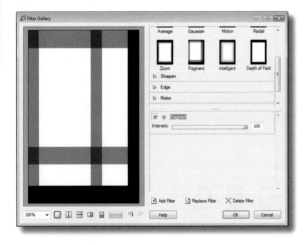

Brushes 5

Brush Tips

The **Brush Tip** tab lets you choose and customize brush tips for the painting tools, define custom brushes, and import Paint Shop Pro 'picture tubes.'

The tab displays a large collection of brushes grouped into various categories, accessible via the drop-down list. Each sample shows the brush tip and stroke; the number indicates the brush diameter. Click a brush tip sample to select it. When any brush-based tool is chosen, the current brush is displayed as a sample on the Context toolbar and in the **Brush Options** dialog.

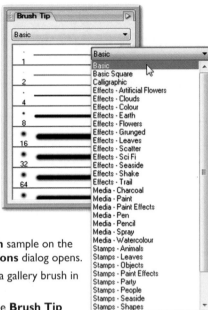

Context toolbar

To customize the current brush, click its **Brush** sample on the Context toolbar (see below). The **Brush Options** dialog opens.

After customizing the brush, you can save it as a gallery brush in a *user-created category*:

1. To add a new user-created category, click the **Brush Tip Tab Menu** arrow button (in the upper right corner of the tab), and select **Add Category**.

2. When you've created your category, it displays automatically in the category drop-down list. Right-click in the gallery and select **New Brush**.

3. Name your brush and then click **OK**. Your new brush is added to your new user-created category.

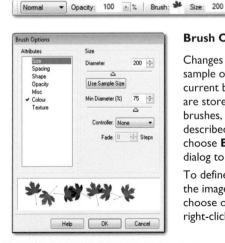

Brush Options

Changes you make to the current brush via the Brush sample on the the Context toolbar only affect the current brush. Brushes in the **Brush Tip** tab galleries are stored separately. To change one of these gallery brushes, first add it to your own category (as described above), then right-click its sample and choose **Brush Options**. Use the **Brush Options** dialog to alter the properties of the brush.

To define a custom brush using a shape or a portion of the image, first make a selection in the image, then choose one of your own user-created categories, right-click in the gallery, and choose **Define Brush**.

Basic/Basic Square

Basic
Round01
(1 pixel dia.)

Basic
Round02
(2 pixels dia.)

Basic
Round03
(4 pixels dia.)

Basic
Round04
(8 pixels dia.)

Basic
Round05
(16 pixels dia.)

Basic
Round06
(32 pixels dia.)

Basic
Round07
(64 pixels dia.)

Basic
Round08
(128 pixels dia.)

Basic
Round09
(256 pixels dia.)

Basic
Round Hard01
(1 pixels dia.)

Basic
Round Hard02
(2 pixels dia.)

Basic
Round Hard03
(4 pixels dia.)

Basic
Round Hard04
(8 pixels dia.)

Basic
Round Hard05
(16 pixels dia.)

Basic
Round Hard06
(32 pixels dia.)

Basic
Round Hard07
(64 pixels dia.)

Basic
Round Hard08
(128 pixels dia.)

Basic
Round Hard09
(256 pixels dia.)

Basic Square
Square01
(1 pixels dia.)

Basic Square
Square02
(2 pixels dia.)

Basic Square
Square03
(4 pixels dia.)

Basic Square/Calligraphic

Basic Square
Square04
(8 pixels dia.)

Basic Square
Square05
(16 pixels dia.)

Basic Square
Square06
(32 pixels dia.)

Basic Square
Square07
(64 pixels dia.)

Basic Square
Square08
(128 pixels dia.)

Basic Square
Square09
(256 pixels dia.)

Basic Square
Square Hard01
(1 pixels dia.)

Basic Square
Square Hard02
(2 pixels dia.)

Basic Square
Square Hard03
(4 pixels dia.)

Basic Square
Square Hard04
(8 pixels dia.)

Basic Square
Square Hard05
(16 pixels dia.)

Basic Square
Square Hard06
(32 pixels dia.)

Basic Square
Square Hard07
(64 pixels dia.)

Basic Square
Square Hard08
(128 pixels dia.)

Basic Square
Square Hard09
(256 pixels dia.)

Calligraphic
Calligraphic Soft01
(10 pixels dia.)

Calligraphic
Calligraphic Soft02
(25 pixels dia.)

Calligraphic
Calligraphic Soft03
(50 pixels dia.)

Calligraphic
Calligraphic Soft05
(200 pixels dia.)

Calligraphic
Calligraphic Soft04
(100 pixels dia.)

Calligraphic
Calligraphic Hard01
(128 pixels dia.)

Calligraphic/Effects - Artificial Flowers

Calligraphic
Calligraphic Hard02
(25 pixels dia.)

Calligraphic
Calligraphic Hard03
(50 pixels dia.)

Calligraphic
Calligraphic Hard04
(100 pixels dia.)

Calligraphic
Calligraphic Hard05
(200 pixels dia.)

Calligraphic
Calligraphic Rounded Hard01
(10 pixels dia.)

Calligraphic
Calligraphic Rounded Hard02
(25 pixels dia.)

Calligraphic
Calligraphic Rounded Hard03
(50 pixels dia.)

Calligraphic
Calligraphic Rounded
Hard04
(100 pixels dia.)

Calligraphic
Calligraphic Rounded Hard05
(200 pixels dia.)

Calligraphic
Calligraphic Hard Left01
(10 pixels dia.)

Calligraphic
Calligraphic Hard Left02
(25 pixels dia.)

Calligraphic
Calligraphic Hard Left03
(50 pixels dia.)

Calligraphic
Calligraphic Hard Left04
(100 pixels dia.)

Calligraphic
Calligraphic Hard Left05
(200 pixels dia.)

Effects - Artificial Flowers
Rose 01
(200 pixels dia.)

Effects - Artificial Flowers
Rose 02
(200 pixels dia.)

Effects - Artificial Flowers
Rose 03
(200 pixels dia.)

Effects - Artificial Flowers
Rose 04
(200 pixels dia.)

Effects - Artificial Flowers
Rose 05
(200 pixels dia.)

Effects - Artificial Flowers
Butterfly
(200 pixels dia.)

Effects - Artificial Flowers
Butterfly 02
(200 pixels dia.)

Effects - Clouds/Effects - Colour/Effects - Earth

Effects - Clouds
Cloud01
(321 pixels dia.)

Effects - Clouds
Cloud02
(47 pixels dia.)

Effects - Clouds
Cloud03
(47 pixels dia.)

Effects - Clouds
Cloud04
(110 pixels dia.)

Effects - Clouds
Cloud05
(128 pixels dia.)

Effects - Clouds
Cloud06
(128 pixels dia.)

Effects - Clouds
Cloud07
(156 pixels dia.)

Effects - Clouds
Cloud08
(128 pixels dia.)

Effects - Clouds
Cloud09
(128 pixels dia.)

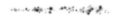

Effects - Colour
Colour01
(10 pixels dia.)

Effects - Colour
Colour02
(10 pixels dia.)

Effects - Colour
Colour03
(100 pixels dia.)

Effects - Colour
Colour04
(100 pixels dia.)

Effects - Colour
Colour05
(200 pixels dia.)

Effects - Colour
Colour06
(200 pixels dia.)

Effects - Colour
Colour07
(25 pixels dia.)

Effects - Colour
Colour08
(25 pixels dia.)

Effects - Colour
Colour09
(50 pixels dia.)

Effects - Colour
Colour10
(50 pixels dia.)

Effects - Colour
Colour11
(50 pixels dia.)

Effects - Earth
Blade of Grass01
(128 pixels dia.)

Effects - Earth/Effects - Flowers/Effects - Grunged

Effects - Earth
Blade of Grass02
(128 pixels dia.)

Effects - Earth
Blade of Grass03
(128 pixels dia.)

Effects - Earth
Blade of Grass04
(128 pixels dia.)

Effects - Earth
Branch01
(128 pixels dia.)

Effects - Earth
Branch02
(128 pixels dia.)

Effects - Earth
Leaf01
(128 pixels dia.)

Effects - Earth
Leaf02
(128 pixels dia.)

Effects - Earth
Leaf03
(128 pixels dia.)

Effects - Earth
Leaf04
(128 pixels dia.)

Effects - Flowers
Carnation 01
(200 pixels dia.)

Effects - Flowers
Carnation 02
(200 pixels dia.)

Effects - Flowers
Carnation 03
(200 pixels dia.)

Effects - Flowers
Daisy 01
(200 pixels dia.)

Effects - Flowers
Daisy 02
(200 pixels dia.)

Effects - Flowers
Daisy 03
(200 pixels dia.)

Effects - Flowers
Daisy 04
(200 pixels dia.)

Effects - Flowers
Daisy 05
(200 pixels dia.)

Effects - Flowers
Daisy 06
(200 pixels dia.)

Effects - Flowers
Flower 01
(200 pixels dia.)

Effects - Flowers
Gerbera 01
(200 pixels dia.)

Effects - Grunged
Grunged01
(500 pixels dia.)

Effects - Grunged

Effects - Grunged
Grunged02
(500 pixels dia.)

Effects - Grunged
Grunged03
(449 pixels dia.)

Effects - Grunged
Tape01
(400 pixels dia.)

Effects - Grunged
Tape02
(400 pixels dia.)

Effects - Grunged
Crumple
(500 pixels dia.)

Effects - Grunged
Crumple Fade
(500 pixels dia.)

Effects - Grunged
Corner Crumple
(500 pixels dia.)

Effects - Grunged
Crease
(500 pixels dia.)

Effects - Grunged
Creased Line
(496 pixels dia.)

Effects - Grunged
Dots
(500 pixels dia.)

Effects - Grunged
Blot01
(150 pixels dia.)

Effects - Grunged
Blot02
(200 pixels dia.)

Effects - Grunged
Blot03
(200 pixels dia.)

Effects - Grunged
Blot04
(150 pixels dia.)

Effects - Grunged
Blot05
(200 pixels dia.)

Effects - Grunged
Blot06
(200 pixels dia.)

Effects - Grunged
Blot07
(200 pixels dia.)

Effects - Grunged
Blot08
(50 pixels dia.)

Effects - Grunged
Blot09
(150 pixels dia.)

Effects - Grunged
Blot10
(200 pixels dia.)

Effects - Grunged
Blot11
(200 pixels dia.)

Effects - Grunged/Effects - Leaves/Effects - Scatter

Effects - Grunged
Blot12
(200 pixels dia.)

Effects - Grunged
Blot13
(50 pixels dia.)

Effects - Grunged
Blot14
(200 pixels dia.)

Effects - Leaves
Rowan 1
(200 pixels dia.)

Effects - Leaves
Rowan 2
(200 pixels dia.)

Effects - Leaves
Rowan 3
(200 pixels dia.)

Effects - Leaves
Rowan 4
(200 pixels dia.)

Effects - Leaves
Maple 1
(200 pixels dia.)

Effects - Leaves
Maple 2
(200 pixels dia.)

Effects - Leaves
Shrub 1
(200 pixels dia.)

Effects - Leaves
Shrub 2
(200 pixels dia.)

Effects - Scatter
Cross01
(10 pixels dia.)

Effects - Scatter
Cross02
(25 pixels dia.)

Effects - Scatter
Cross03
(50 pixels dia.)

Effects - Scatter
Cross04
(100 pixels dia.)

Effects - Scatter
Cross05
(200 pixels dia.)

Effects - Scatter
Straws01
(10 pixels dia.)

Effects - Scatter
Straws02
(25 pixels dia.)

Effects - Scatter
Straws03
(50 pixels dia.)

Effects - Scatter
Straws04
(100 pixels dia.)

Effects - Scatter
Straws05
(200 pixels dia.)

Effects - Scatter/Effects - Sci-Fi/Effects - Seaside

Effects - Scatter
Wild01
(10 pixels dia.)

Effects - Scatter
Wild02
(25 pixels dia.)

Effects - Scatter
Wild03
(50 pixels dia.)

Effects - Scatter
Wild04
(100 pixels dia.)

Effects - Scatter
Wild05
(200 pixels dia.)

Effects - Scatter
Wild Scatter01
(10 pixels dia.)

Effects - Scatter
Wild Scatter02
(25 pixels dia.)

Effects - Scatter
Wild Scatter03
(50 pixels dia.)

Effects - Scatter
Wild Scatter04
(100 pixels dia.)

Effects - Scatter
Wild Scatter05
(200 pixels dia.)

Effects - Sci-Fi
Sci-fi 01
(197 pixels dia.)

Effects - Sci-Fi
Sci-fi 02
(85 pixels dia.)

Effects - Sci-Fi
Sci-fi 03
(150 pixels dia.)

Effects - Sci-Fi
Sci-fi 04
(280 pixels dia.)

Effects - Sci-Fi
Sci-fi 05
(99 pixels dia.)

Effects - Sci-Fi
Sci-fi 06
(82 pixels dia.)

Effects - Sci-Fi
Sci-fi 07
(177 pixels dia.)

Effects - Sci-Fi
Sci-fi 08
(251 pixels dia.)

Effects - Sci-Fi
Sci-fi 09
(106 pixels dia.)

Effects - Seaside
Shell 1
(200 pixels dia.)

Effects - Seaside
Shell 1 Inside
(200 pixels dia.)

Effects - Seaside//Effects - Shake//Effects - Trail

Effects - Seaside
Shell 2
(200 pixels dia.)

Effects - Seaside
Shell 2 Inside
(200 pixels dia.)

Effects - Seaside
Shell 3
(200 pixels dia.)

Effects - Seaside
Shell 3 Inside
(200 pixels dia.)

Effects - Seaside
Shell 4
(200 pixels dia.)

Effects - Seaside
Shell 4 Inside
(200 pixels dia.)

Effects - Seaside
Shell 5
(200 pixels dia.)

Effects - Seaside
Shell 5 Inside
(200 pixels dia.)

Effects - Seaside
Sea Urchin
(200 pixels dia.)

Effects - Seaside
Sea Urchin Inside
(200 pixels dia.)

Effects - Shake
Shake01
(128 pixels dia.)

Effects - Shake
Shake02
(128 pixels dia.)

Effects - Shake
Shake03
(128 pixels dia.)

Effects - Shake
Shake04
(128 pixels dia.)

Effects - Shake
Shake05
(128 pixels dia.)

Effects - Shake
Shake06
(128 pixels dia.)

Effects - Shake
Shake07
(128 pixels dia.)

Effects - Shake
Shake08
(128 pixels dia.)

Effects - Trail
Trail01
(19 pixels dia.)

Effects - Trail
Trail02
(19 pixels dia.)

Effects - Trail
Trail03
(19 pixels dia.)

Effects - Trail/Media - Charcoal/Media- Paint

Effects - Trail
Trail04
(19 pixels dia.)

Effects - Trail
Trail05
(19 pixels dia.)

Effects - Trail
Trail06
(19 pixels dia.)

Effects - Trail
Trail07
(19 pixels dia.)

Effects - Trail
Trail08
(32 pixels dia.)

Effects - Trail
Trail09
(32 pixels dia.)

Effects - Trail
Trail10
(32 pixels dia.)

Effects - Trail
Trail11
(32 pixels dia.)

Effects - Trail
Trail12
(32 pixels dia.)

Media - Charcoal
Charcoal 01
(12 pixels dia.)

Media - Charcoal
Charcoal 02
(15 pixels dia.)

Media - Charcoal
Charcoal 03
(10 pixels dia.)

Media - Charcoal
Charcoal 04
(15 pixels dia.)

Media - Charcoal
Charcoal 05
(50 pixels dia.)

Media - Charcoal
Charcoal 06
(15 pixels dia.)

Media - Charcoal
Charcoal 07
(100 pixels dia.)

Media - Charcoal
Charcoal 08
(60 pixels dia.)

Media - Charcoal
Charcoal 09
(15 pixels dia.)

Media - Charcoal
Charcoal 10
(10 pixels dia.)

Media - Charcoal
Charcoal 11
(30 pixels dia.)

Media - Paint
Paint 01
(30 pixels dia.)

Media - Paint/Media - Paint Effects

Media - Paint
Paint 02
(64 pixels dia.)

Media - Paint
Paint 03
(80 pixels dia.)

Media - Paint
Paint 04
(120 pixels dia.)

Media - Paint
Paint 05
(40 pixels dia.)

Media - Paint
Paint 06
(130 pixels dia.)

Media - Paint
Paint 07
(50 pixels dia.)

Media - Paint
Paint 08
(60 pixels dia.)

Media - Paint
Paint 09
(100 pixels dia.)

Media - Paint
Paint 10
(50 pixels dia.)

Media - Paint
Paint 11
(60 pixels dia.)

Media - Paint
Paint 12
(40 pixels dia.)

Media - Paint
Paint 13
(100 pixels dia.)

Media - Paint
Paint 14
(40 pixels dia.)

Media - Paint
Paint 15
(50 pixels dia.)

Media - Paint
Paint 16
(40 pixels dia.)

Media - Paint
Paint 17
(50 pixels dia.)

Media - Paint
Paint 18
(70 pixels dia.)

Media - Paint
Paint 19
(40 pixels dia.)

Media - Paint Effects
Chalk Dabs
(236 pixels dia.)

Media - Paint Effects
Chalk
(22 pixels dia.)

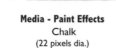

Media - Paint Effects
Charcoal
(3 pixels dia.)

Media - Paint Effects

Media - Paint Effects
Colour Pencil01
(3 pixels dia.)

Media - Paint Effects
Crackle Glaze
(64 pixels dia.)

Media - Paint Effects
Heavy Charcoal
(29 pixels dia.)

Media - Paint Effects
Heavy Pencil
(2 pixels dia.)

Media - Paint Effects
Oil Crayon
(3 pixels dia.)

Media - Paint Effects
Paint Dab01
(32 pixels dia.)

Media - Paint Effects
Paint Dab02
(21 pixels dia.)

Media - Paint Effects
Paint Dabs03
(21 pixels dia.)

Media - Paint Effects
Pen Hatch Mix
(8 pixels dia.)

Media - Paint Effects
Pen Hatch Random
(8 pixels dia.)

Media - Paint Effects
Pen Hatch
(32 pixels dia.)

Media - Paint Effects
Pen Line Variant
(8 pixels dia.)

Media - Paint Effects
Pen Vertical
(8 pixels dia.)

Media - Paint Effects
Soft Pencil
(3 pixels dia.)

Media - Paint Effects
Watercolour Dab
(32 pixels dia.)

Media - Paint Effects
Watercolour
(32 pixels dia.)

Media - Paint Effects
Wax Crayon
(3 pixels dia.)

Media - Paint Effects
Wide Chalk
(22 pixels dia.)

Media - Paint Effects
Sponge01
(10 pixels dia.)

Media - Paint Effects
Sponge02
(25 pixels dia.)

Media - Paint Effects
Sponge03
(50 pixels dia.)

Media - Paint Effects/Media - Pen/Media - Pencil

Media - Paint Effects
Sponge04
(100 pixels dia.)

Media - Paint Effects
Sponge05
(200 pixels dia.)

Media - Pen
Pen Hatch 01
(24 pixels dia.)

Media - Pen
Pen 01
(128 pixels dia.)

Media - Pen
Pen 02
(127 pixels dia.)

Media - Pen
Pen 03
(64 pixels dia.)

Media - Pen
Pen 04
(128 pixels dia.)

Media - Pen
Pen 05
(128 pixels dia.)

Media - Pen
Pen 06
(5 pixels dia.)

Media - Pen
Pen Hatch 02
(128 pixels dia.)

Media - Pen
Pen 07
(8 pixels dia.)

Media - Pen
Pen 08
(8 pixels dia.)

Media - Pen
Pen 09
(254 pixels dia.)

Media - Pen
Pen 10
(12 pixels dia.)

Media - Pencil
Pencil 01
(130 pixels dia.)

Media - Pencil
Pencil 02
(5 pixels dia.)

Media - Pencil
Pencil Scribble 01
(128 pixels dia.)

Media - Pencil
Pencil Scribble 02
(128 pixels dia.)

Media - Pencil
Pencil Scribble 03
(128 pixels dia.)

Media - Pencil
Pencil Scribble 04
(128 pixels dia.)

Media - Pencil
Pencil 03
(127 pixels dia.)

Media - Pencil
Pencil 04
(126 pixels dia.)

Media - Pencil
Pencil 05
(8 pixels dia.)

Media - Pencil
Pencil 06
(15 pixels dia.)

Media - Pencil
Pencil Hatch 01
(128 pixels dia.)

Media - Pencil
Pencil Hatch 02
(128 pixels dia.)

Media - Pencil
Pencil 07
(28 pixels dia.)

Media - Pencil
Pencil 08
(24 pixels dia.)

Media - Spray
Horizontal01
(10 pixels dia.)

Media - Spray
Horizontal02
(25 pixels dia.)

Media - Spray
Horizontal03
(50 pixels dia.)

Media - Spray
Horizontal04
(100 pixels dia.)

Media - Spray
Horizontal05
(200 pixels dia.)

Media - Spray
Scatter Hard01
(10 pixels dia.)

Media - Spray
Scatter Hard02
(25 pixels dia.)

Media - Spray
Scatter Hard03
(50 pixels dia.)

Media - Spray
Scatter Hard04
(100 pixels dia.)

Media - Spray
Scatter Hard05
(200 pixels dia.)

Media - Spray
Scatter Soft01
(10 pixels dia.)

Media - Spray
Scatter Soft02
(25 pixels dia.)

Media - Spray
Scatter Soft03
(50 pixels dia.)

Media - Spray
Scatter Soft04
(100 pixels dia.)

Media - Spray/Media - Watercolour

Media - Spray
Scatter Soft05
(200 pixels dia.)

Media - Spray
Sponge Spray01
(10 pixels dia.)

Media - Spray
Sponge Spray02
(25 pixels dia.)

Media - Spray
Sponge Spray03
(50 pixels dia.)

Media - Spray
Sponge Spray04
(100 pixels dia.)

Media - Spray
Sponge Spray05
(200 pixels dia.)

Media - Spray
Tight Spray01
(10 pixels dia.)

Media - Spray
Tight Spray02
(25 pixels dia.)

Media - Spray
Tight Spray03
(50 pixels dia.)

Media - Spray
Tight Spray04
(100 pixels dia.)

Media - Spray
Tight Spray05
(200 pixels dia.)

Media - Spray
Vertical01
(10 pixels dia.)

Media - Spray
Vertical02
(25 pixels dia.)

Media - Spray
Vertical03
(50 pixels dia.)

Media - Spray
Vertical04
(100 pixels dia.)

Media - Spray
Vertical05
(200 pixels dia.)

Media - Watercolour
Watercolour 1
(128 pixels dia.)

Media - Watercolour
Watercolour 2
(128 pixels dia.)

Media - Watercolour
Watercolour 3
(128 pixels dia.)

Media - Watercolour
Watercolour 4
(128 pixels dia.)

Media - Watercolour
Watercolour 5
(128 pixels dia.)

Media - Watercolour

Media - Watercolour
Watercolour 6
(128 pixels dia.)

Media - Watercolour
Watercolour 7
(128 pixels dia.)

Media - Watercolour
Watercolour 8
(128 pixels dia.)

Media - Watercolour
Watercolour 9
(128 pixels dia.)

Media - Watercolour
Watercolour 10
(128 pixels dia.)

Media - Watercolour
Watercolour 11
(128 pixels dia.)

Media - Watercolour
Watercolour 12
(128 pixels dia.)

Media - Watercolour
Watercolour 13
(128 pixels dia.)

Media - Watercolour
Watercolour 14
(128 pixels dia.)

Media - Watercolour
Watercolour 15
(128 pixels dia.)

Media - Watercolour
Watercolour 16
(128 pixels dia.)

Media - Watercolour
Watercolour 17
(128 pixels dia.)

Media - Watercolour
Watercolour 18
(128 pixels dia.)

Media - Watercolour
Watercolour 19
(128 pixels dia.)

Media - Watercolour
Watercolour 20
(128 pixels dia.)

Media - Watercolour
Watercolour 21
(128 pixels dia.)

Media - Watercolour
Watercolour 22
(128 pixels dia.)

Media - Watercolour
Watercolour 23
(128 pixels dia.)

Media - Watercolour
Watercolour 24
(128 pixels dia.)

Stamps - Animals/Leaves/Objects

Stamps - Animals
Horse
(200 pixels dia.)

Stamps - Animals
Dog
(200 pixels dia.)

Stamps - Animals
Cat
(200 pixels dia.)

Stamps - Animals
Bird
(200 pixels dia.)

Stamps - Animals
Lizard
(200 pixels dia.)

Stamps - Animals
Butterfly
(200 pixels dia.)

Stamps - Animals
Fish
(200 pixels dia.)

Stamps - Animals
Cat Paw
(110 pixels dia.)

Stamps - Animals
Bird Print
(140 pixels dia.)

Stamps - Animals
Dog Paw
(110 pixels dia.)

Stamps - Leaves
Leaf 1
(300 pixels dia.)

Stamps - Leaves
Leaf 2
(300 pixels dia.)

Stamps - Leaves
Rowan 1
(200 pixels dia.)

Stamps - Leaves
Rowan 2
(200 pixels dia.)

Stamps - Leaves
Rowan 3
(200 pixels dia.)

Stamps - Leaves
Rowan 4
(200 pixels dia.)

Stamps - Leaves
Maple 1
(200 pixels dia.)

Stamps - Leaves
Maple 2
(200 pixels dia.)

Stamps - Leaves
Ash 1
(200 pixels dia.)

Stamps - Leaves
Ash 2
(200 pixels dia.)

Stamps - Leaves
Ash 3
(200 pixels dia.)

Stamps - Leaves
Ash 4
(200 pixels dia.)

Stamps - Leaves
Horse Chestnut
1
(200 pixels dia.)

Stamps - Leaves
Horse Chestnut
2

Stamps - Leaves
Sycamore 1
(200 pixels dia.)

Stamps - Leaves
Sycamore 2
(200 pixels dia.)

Stamps - Leaves
Sycamore 3
(200 pixels dia.)

Stamps - Leaves
Shrub 1
(200 pixels dia.)

Stamps - Objects
Ying Yang
(200 pixels dia.)

Stamps - Objects
Sun
(200 pixels dia.)

Stamps - Objects/Paint Effects/Party/People

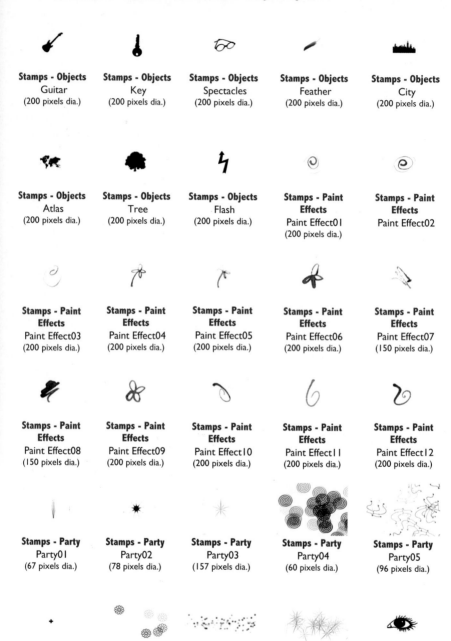

Stamps - Objects
Guitar
(200 pixels dia.)

Stamps - Objects
Key
(200 pixels dia.)

Stamps - Objects
Spectacles
(200 pixels dia.)

Stamps - Objects
Feather
(200 pixels dia.)

Stamps - Objects
City
(200 pixels dia.)

Stamps - Objects
Atlas
(200 pixels dia.)

Stamps - Objects
Tree
(200 pixels dia.)

Stamps - Objects
Flash
(200 pixels dia.)

**Stamps - Paint
Effects**
Paint Effect01
(200 pixels dia.)

**Stamps - Paint
Effects**
Paint Effect02

**Stamps - Paint
Effects**
Paint Effect03
(200 pixels dia.)

**Stamps - Paint
Effects**
Paint Effect04
(200 pixels dia.)

**Stamps - Paint
Effects**
Paint Effect05
(200 pixels dia.)

**Stamps - Paint
Effects**
Paint Effect06
(200 pixels dia.)

**Stamps - Paint
Effects**
Paint Effect07
(150 pixels dia.)

**Stamps - Paint
Effects**
Paint Effect08
(150 pixels dia.)

**Stamps - Paint
Effects**
Paint Effect09
(200 pixels dia.)

**Stamps - Paint
Effects**
Paint Effect10
(200 pixels dia.)

**Stamps - Paint
Effects**
Paint Effect11
(200 pixels dia.)

**Stamps - Paint
Effects**
Paint Effect12
(200 pixels dia.)

Stamps - Party
Party01
(67 pixels dia.)

Stamps - Party
Party02
(78 pixels dia.)

Stamps - Party
Party03
(157 pixels dia.)

Stamps - Party
Party04
(60 pixels dia.)

Stamps - Party
Party05
(96 pixels dia.)

Stamps - Party
Party06
(50 pixels dia.)

Stamps - Party
Party07
(51 pixels dia.)

Stamps - Party
Party08
(8 pixels dia.)

Stamps - Party
Party09
(157 pixels dia.)

Stamps - People
Eye
(100 pixels dia.)

Stamps - People/Seaside/Shapes/Splats/Transport

Stamps - People
Female Face
(250 pixels dia.)

Stamps - People
Male Face
(200 pixels dia.)

Stamps - People
Jogging
(200 pixels dia.)

Stamps - People
Footballer
(200 pixels dia.)

Stamps - People
Rambler
(200 pixels dia.)

Stamps - People
Lips
(200 pixels dia.)

Stamps - People
Business
Woman

Stamps - People
Business Man
(200 pixels dia.)

Stamps - People
Hand
(200 pixels dia.)

Stamps - People
Crowd
(200 pixels dia.)

Stamps - Seaside
Shell 1
(200 pixels dia.)

Stamps - Seaside
Shell 2
(200 pixels dia.)

Stamps - Seaside
Shell 3
(200 pixels dia.)

Stamps - Seaside
Shell 4
(200 pixels dia.)

Stamps - Seaside
Shell 5
(200 pixels dia.)

Stamps - Seaside
Sea Urchin
(200 pixels dia.)

Stamps - Shapes
Stamp01
(151 pixels dia.)

Stamps - Shapes
Stamp02
(108 pixels dia.)

Stamps - Shapes
Stamp03
(82 pixels dia.)

Stamps - Shapes
Stamp04
(82 pixels dia.)

Stamps - Shapes
Stamp05
(82 pixels dia.)

Stamps - Shapes
Stamp06
(151 pixels dia.)

Stamps - Splats
Splat Stamp 01
(200 pixels dia.)

Stamps - Splats
Splat Stamp 02
(150 pixels dia.)

Stamps - Splats
Splat Stamp 03
(150 pixels dia.)

Stamps - Splats
Splat Stamp 04
(150 pixels dia.)

Stamps - Splats
Splat Stamp 05
(300 pixels dia.)

**Stamps -
Transport**
Motorbike
(200 pixels dia.)

**Stamps -
Transport**
Car
(200 pixels dia.)

**Stamps -
Transport**
Bicycle
(200 pixels dia.)

Stamps - Transport/Wires & Picture Brushes

Stamps - Transport
Tram

Stamps - Transport
Airship
(200 pixels dia.)

Stamps - Transport
Aeroplane01
(200 pixels dia.)

Stamps - Transport
Aeroplane02
(200 pixels dia.)

Stamps - Transport
Sailboat

Stamps - Transport
Helicopter

Stamps - Transport
Scooter

Stamps - Wires
Wires01
(500 pixels dia.)

Stamps - Wires
Wires02
(50 pixels dia.)

Stamps - Wires
Wires03
(50 pixels dia.)

Stamps - Wires
Wires04
(73 pixels dia.)

Picture Brushes

Confetti
Confetti Circles

Confetti
Confetti Hearts

Confetti
Confetti
Horseshoe

Confetti
Confetti Squares

Confetti
Confetti Stars

Simple
Blue Tube

Simple
Coloured Tube

Simple
Gold Tube

Simple
Green Tube

Simple
Luminous Tube

Simple
Magenta Tube

Simple
Orange Tube

Simple
Purple Tube

Simple
Red Tube

Simple
Sea Green Tube

Picture Brushes

Simple
Silver Tube

Spirals and Stars
Blue Corkscrew

Spirals and Stars
Blue Stars

Spirals and Stars
Green
Corkscrew

Spirals and Stars
Multi Swirls

Spirals and Stars
Red Burn Stars

Spirals and Stars
Red Multi Stars

Spirals and Stars
Red Corkscrew

Spirals and Stars
Shiny Spirals

Spirals and Stars
Sparkle

Spirals and Stars
Steel Corkscrew

Spirals and Stars
Tropical Carpet

Splat
Arcade

Splat
Camouflage01

Splat
Camouflage02

Splat
Camouflage03

Splat
Camouflage04

Splat
Dots

Splat
Green Splot
Tube

Splat
Gunge

Splat
Multi-spots

Splat
Purple Splot
Tube

Splat
Red Splot Tube

Image
Collection

6

Image Collection

PhotoPlus includes a collection of images that you can use in your own creations—for example, as a starting point for a new image, as a background for one of your own photographs, or incorporated into a Web site or collage.

The **Image Collection** is available on the **Studio Extras DVD**.

To access the **Image Collection**, go to **File** and then choose **Browse Image Collection...**

You can also access other resources on the **Studio Extras DVD** from the **File** menu such as **Photo Frames**, **Samples** and **Scrapbook** images.

Animals and Wildlife

Animals and Wildlife
15964799.jpg

Animals and Wildlife
30423124.jpg

Animals and Wildlife
30423146.jpg

Animals and Wildlife
30445853.jpg

Animals and Wildlife
30477480.jpg

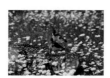
Animals and Wildlife
30477513.jpg

Animals and Wildlife
30477744.jpg

Animals and Wildlife
30479581.jpg

Animals and Wildlife
30479680.jpg

Animals and Wildlife
30480604.jpg

Animals and Wildlife
30481176.jpg

Animals and Wildlife
30482936.jpg

Animals and Wildlife
30494372.jpg

Animals and Wildlife
30540108.jpg

Animals and Wildlife
30540867.jpg

Animals and Wildlife
34650917.jpg

Animals and Wildlife
34696941.jpg

Animals and Wildlife
34697111.jpg

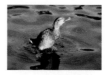
Animals and Wildlife
34803438.jpg

Animals and Wildlife
34804657.jpg

Animals and Wildlife/Architecture

Animals and Wildlife
34843916.jpg

Animals and Wildlife
34845134.jpg

Animals and Wildlife
34859257.jpg

Animals and Wildlife
34877284.jpg

Animals and Wildlife
37694784.jpg

Animals and Wildlife
37765293.jpg

Animals and Wildlife
37765306.jpg

Animals and Wildlife
37784143.jpg

Animals and Wildlife
37795791.jpg

Animals and Wildlife
37799457.jpg

Animals and Wildlife
37812379.jpg

Animals and Wildlife
37819425.jpg

Animals and Wildlife
37833959.jpg

Animals and Wildlife
37859686.jpg

Animals and Wildlife
38078243.jpg

Animals and Wildlife
7654326.jpg

Animals and Wildlife
7656254.jpg

Architecture
34807542.jpg

Architecture
34807793.jpg

Architecture
34808057.jpg

Architecture

Architecture
34821561.jpg

Architecture
34821802.jpg

Architecture
34830097.jpg

Architecture
34831075.jpg

Architecture
34831230.jpg

Architecture
34848555.jpg

Architecture
34849149.jpg

Architecture
34854374.jpg

Architecture
34888797.jpg

Architecture
34891448.jpg

Architecture
35319486.jpg

Architecture
37692262.jpg

Architecture
37692691.jpg

Architecture
37693809.jpg

Architecture
37693952.jpg

Architecture
37694355.jpg

Architecture
37694381.jpg

Architecture
37694459.jpg

Architecture
37694550.jpg

Architecture
37694667.jpg

Architecture/Backgrounds

Architecture
37694693.jpg

Architecture
37694706.jpg

Architecture
37767724.jpg

Backgrounds
14497649.jpg

Backgrounds
19155377.jpg

Backgrounds
19224277.jpg

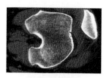

Backgrounds
19239139.jpg

Backgrounds
19256076.jpg

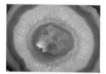

Backgrounds
19300377.jpg

Backgrounds
19302475.jpg

Backgrounds
30444522.jpg

Backgrounds
30445677.jpg

Backgrounds
30754873.jpg

Backgrounds
32339204.jpg

Backgrounds
34730736.jpg

Backgrounds
34798993.jpg

Backgrounds
34850546.jpg

Backgrounds
34880613.jpg

Backgrounds
36595645.jpg

Backgrounds
36597478.jpg

Backgrounds/Finance

Backgrounds
36599909.jpg

Backgrounds
36607332.jpg

Backgrounds
9869622.jpg

Finance
16450004.jpg

Finance
19085127.jpg

Finance
19092432.jpg

Finance
19092454.jpg

Finance
19092467.jpg

Finance
19099207.jpg

Finance
19147040.jpg

Finance
19147631.jpg

Finance
19151044.jpg

Finance
19158815.jpg

Finance
19279230.jpg

Finance
19392773.jpg

Finance
24722238.jpg

Finance
32313730.jpg

Finance
32351819.jpg

Finance
32351863.jpg

Finance
3693646.jpg

Finance/Food and Drink

Finance
37899062.jpg

Finance
4890511.jpg

Finance
4890573.jpg

Finance
5236795.jpg

Finance
5244250.jpg

Finance
5259218.jpg

Finance
7231906.jpg

Finance
7232493.jpg

Finance
7232600.jpg

Food and Drink
16320195.jpg

Food and Drink
27376441.jpg

Food and Drink
27378055.jpg

Food and Drink
27378348.jpg

Food and Drink
2804551.jpg

Food and Drink
30453586.jpg

Food and Drink
30882126.jpg

Food and Drink
37692379.jpg

Food and Drink
37704599.jpg

Food and Drink
37729623.jpg

Food and Drink
37731508.jpg

Food and Drink

Food and Drink
37778072.jpg

Food and Drink
37899933.jpg

Food and Drink
37900089.jpg

Food and Drink
37900115.jpg

Food and Drink
5317255.jpg

Food and Drink
5319936.jpg

Food and Drink
5319998.jpg

Food and Drink
5322007.jpg

Food and Drink
5322138.jpg

Food and Drink
5322150.jpg

Food and Drink
5322559.jpg

Food and Drink
5322588.jpg

Food and Drink
5322933.jpg

Food and Drink
5326187.jpg

Food and Drink
5331087.jpg

Food and Drink
5342275.jpg

Food and Drink
5342727.jpg

Food and Drink
5342728.jpg

Food and Drink
5344561.jpg

Food and Drink
5344597.jpg

Food and Drink/Health Care

Food and Drink
5344920.jpg

Food and Drink
5345717.jpg

Food and Drink
5352464.jpg

Food and Drink
5352698.jpg

Food and Drink
5352711.jpg

Food and Drink
5352732.jpg

Food and Drink
5352743.jpg

Food and Drink
5352766.jpg

Food and Drink
7361406.jpg

Food and Drink
7775025.jpg

Health Care
16353793.jpg

Health Care
16359115.jpg

Health Care
19073837.jpg

Health Care
19085895.jpg

Health Care
19095898.jpg

Health Care
36603055.jpg

Health Care
36603731.jpg

Health Care
37741428.jpg

Health Care
37761588.jpg

Health Care
4559847.jpg

Health Care/Holidays and Occasions

Health Care
5115085.jpg

Health Care
5320004.jpg

Health Care
5322689.jpg

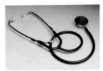

Health Care
5322695.jpg

Health Care
5322706.jpg

Health Care
5322709.jpg

Health Care
5322976.jpg

Health Care
5322989.jpg

Health Care
5325816.jpg

Health Care
5343967.jpg

Health Care
7769471.jpg

Health Care
7805861.jpg

Holidays and Occasions
30409940.jpg

Holidays and Occasions
31089207.jpg

Holidays and Occasions
31089954.jpg

Holidays and Occasions
31090234.jpg

Holidays and Occasions
3169688.jpg

Holidays and Occasions
3203001.jpg

Holidays and Occasions
3211368.jpg

Holidays and Occasions
3212797.jpg

Holidays and Occasions

Holidays and
Occasions
3212974.jpg

Holidays and
Occasions
32336949.jpg

Holidays and
Occasions
32336960.jpg

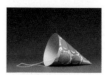

Holidays and
Occasions
3652509.jpg

Holidays and
Occasions
36607306.jpg

Holidays and
Occasions
3663500.jpg

Holidays and
Occasions
3693636.jpg

Holidays and
Occasions
3695508.jpg

Holidays and
Occasions
37467901.jpg

Holidays and
Occasions
37467927.jpg

Holidays and
Occasions
37477144.jpg

Holidays and
Occasions
37812951.jpg

Holidays and
Occasions
37813991.jpg

Holidays and
Occasions
4836235.jpg

Holidays and
Occasions
4836237.jpg

Holidays and
Occasions
4837437.jpg

Holidays and
Occasions
4842604.jpg

Holidays and
Occasions
4842608.jpg

Holidays and
Occasions
5143178.jpg

Holidays and
Occasions
5199841.jpg

Holidays and Occasions/Household Items

**Holidays and
Occasions**
5342471.jpg

**Holidays and
Occasions**
5342594.jpg

**Holidays and
Occasions**
5346062.jpg

Household Items
19082787.jpg

Household Items
19128401.jpg

Household Items
19138016.jpg

Household Items
30363457.jpg

Household Items
31954758.jpg

Household Items
32336212.jpg

Household Items
34613187.jpg

Household Items
34613288.jpg

Household Items
36228046.jpg

Household Items
37476143.jpg

Household Items
37688843.jpg

Household Items
37697137.jpg

Household Items
37697150.jpg

Household Items
37703871.jpg

Household Items
37743105.jpg

Household Items
37743144.jpg

Household Items
37899426.jpg

Household Items/Industry and Agriculture

Household Items
4485606.jpg

Household Items
4865855.jpg

Household Items
4902462.jpg

Household Items
5059481.jpg

Household Items
5201907.jpg

Household Items
5205088.jpg

Household Items
5240680.jpg

Household Items
5301508.jpg

Household Items
5301738.jpg

Household Items
5344559.jpg

Household Items
5352909.jpg

Household Items
9992684.jpg

**Industry and
Agriculture**
2817043.jpg

**Industry and
Agriculture**
30448801.jpg

**Industry and
Agriculture**
3201607.jpg

**Industry and
Agriculture**
3207528.jpg

**Industry and
Agriculture**
3210988.jpg

**Industry and
Agriculture**
37765826.jpg

**Industry and
Agriculture**
37766229.jpg

**Industry and
Agriculture**
37766463.jpg

People

People
19129185.jpg

People
32211204.jpg

People
32259844.jpg

People
32446111.jpg

People
36113361.jpg

People
37693107.jpg

People
37697189.jpg

People
37697696.jpg

People
37698372.jpg

People
37703338.jpg

People
37703741.jpg

People
37704339.jpg

People
37730910.jpg

People
37731586.jpg

People
37731638.jpg

People
37732821.jpg

People
37736951.jpg

People
37740024.jpg

People
37740089.jpg

People
37878627.jpg

People/Religion and Myth

People
37880525.jpg

People
37881006.jpg

People
38068834.jpg

People
5322875.jpg

People
5325429.jpg

People
5325982.jpg

People
5349552.jpg

People
5350504.jpg

Religion and Myth
19266156.jpg

Religion and Myth
24286730.jpg

Religion and Myth
2703083.jpg

Religion and Myth
30360111.jpg

Religion and Myth
3213181.jpg

Religion and Myth
3213728.jpg

Religion and Myth
34706488.jpg

Religion and Myth
34879528.jpg

Religion and Myth
3674923.jpg

Religion and Myth
3695565.jpg

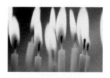
Religion and Myth
4029548.jpg

Religion and Myth
4500592.jpg

Religion and Myth/Science and Technology

Religion and Myth
4518766.jpg

Religion and Myth
4576748.jpg

Religion and Myth
4579201.jpg

Religion and Myth
4642473.jpg

Religion and Myth
4835246.jpg

Religion and Myth
4837441.jpg

Religion and Myth
4837471.jpg

Religion and Myth
4864337.jpg

Religion and Myth
4866101.jpg

Religion and Myth
4866164.jpg

Religion and Myth
4866253.jpg

Religion and Myth
4886995.jpg

Religion and Myth
4893408.jpg

Religion and Myth
5067104.jpg

Religion and Myth
5247902.jpg

Religion and Myth
5250505.jpg

Science and Technology
15610734.jpg

Science and Technology
16010451.jpg

Science and Technology
19075172.jpg

Science and Technology
19094073.jpg

Science and Technology

Science and
Technology
19094145.jpg

Science and
Technology
19158867.jpg

Science and
Technology
19163855.jpg

Science and
Technology
19195988.jpg

Science and
Technology
22473079.jpg

Science and
Technology
24279065.jpg

Science and
Technology
26811588.jpg

Science and
Technology
26812821.jpg

Science and
Technology
30496946.jpg

Science and
Technology
30521278.jpg

Science and
Technology
32313455.jpg

Science and
Technology
32316169.jpg

Science and
Technology
32317936.jpg

Science and
Technology
32352116.jpg

Science and
Technology
34802127.jpg

Science and
Technology
34816072.jpg

Science and
Technology
34901265.jpg

Science and
Technology
37033908.jpg

Science and
Technology
37838379.jpg

Science and
Technology
9826548.jpg

Science and Technology/Signs and Symbols

Science and Technology
9969622.jpg

Signs and Symbols
10002059.jpg

Signs and Symbols
10016362.jpg

Signs and Symbols
19075476.jpg

Signs and Symbols
19172760.jpg

Signs and Symbols
19175246.jpg

Signs and Symbols
19175328.jpg

Signs and Symbols
19175423.jpg

Signs and Symbols
19270538.jpg

Signs and Symbols
30362629.jpg

Signs and Symbols
30362707.jpg

Signs and Symbols
30366349.jpg

Signs and Symbols
30445369.jpg

Signs and Symbols
30516581.jpg

Signs and Symbols
32316224.jpg

Signs and Symbols
32354052.jpg

Signs and Symbols
34612508.jpg

Signs and Symbols
34887774.jpg

Signs and Symbols
34892394.jpg

Signs and Symbols
36594696.jpg

Signs and Symbols/Sports and Recreation

Signs and Symbols
36596074.jpg

Signs and Symbols
36598843.jpg

Signs and Symbols
36606136.jpg

Signs and Symbols
36608528.jpg

Signs and Symbols
36608658.jpg

Signs and Symbols
37471099.jpg

Signs and Symbols
37692600.jpg

Signs and Symbols
37692821.jpg

Signs and Symbols
37700413.jpg

Signs and Symbols
37832542.jpg

Signs and Symbols
37901545.jpg

Sports and Recreation
10035250.jpg

Sports and Recreation
14500036.jpg

Sports and Recreation
19032421.jpg

Sports and Recreation
19054014.jpg

Sports and Recreation
19139187.jpg

Sports and Recreation
19184346.jpg

Sports and Recreation
19189583.jpg

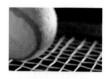

Sports and Recreation
19206627.jpg

Sports and Recreation
19206691.jpg

Sports and Recreation/Transportation

Sports and Recreation
19259091.jpg

Sports and Recreation
19305892.jpg

Sports and Recreation
24267047.jpg

Sports and Recreation
27353083.jpg

Sports and Recreation
30424796.jpg

Sports and Recreation
30426857.jpg

Sports and Recreation
30430186.jpg

Sports and Recreation
30436254.jpg

Sports and Recreation
30438069.jpg

Sports and Recreation
30457623.jpg

Sports and Recreation
34607954.jpg

Sports and Recreation
37835064.jpg

Sports and Recreation
37835246.jpg

Sports and Recreation
37858763.jpg

Sports and Recreation
7333606.jpg

Sports and Recreation
7772153.jpg

Sports and Recreation
7772760.jpg

Transportation
15612042.jpg

Transportation
16318845.jpg

Transportation
19004973.jpg

Transportation

Transportation
19023357.jpg

Transportation
19188289.jpg

Transportation
19211805.jpg

Transportation
19220712.jpg

Transportation
19221041.jpg

Transportation
24256815.jpg

Transportation
24258863.jpg

Transportation
26810998.jpg

Transportation
26813403.jpg

Transportation
30481066.jpg

Transportation
3201581.jpg

Transportation
32225966.jpg

Transportation
34826191.jpg

Transportation
34827060.jpg

Transportation
34828798.jpg

Transportation
34833201.jpg

Transportation
34851492.jpg

Transportation
34877086.jpg

Transportation
36601079.jpg

Transportation
36841465.jpg

Transportation

Transportation
37692834.jpg

Transportation
4486997.jpg

Transportation
4507320.jpg

Transportation
5095566.jpg

Transportation
5095974.jpg

Transportation
5097437.jpg

Transportation
5169342.jpg

Transportation
5169758.jpg

Transportation
5237155.jpg

Transportation
5343996.jpg

Transportation
5344006.jpg

Transportation
5344017.jpg

Transportation
7237377.jpg

Transportation
7613408.jpg

Transportation
7636822.jpg

Transportation
7651053.jpg

Transportation
7689755.jpg

Transportation
7715175.jpg

Transportation
9959631.jpg

Transportation
9992009.jpg